FUTURESCAN

Health Care Trends and Implications

2020–2025

Transformation and Disruption

by Ian Morrison, Ph.D.

Once again, the Society for Health Care Strategy & Market Development (SHSMD) and the American College of Healthcare Executives have curated a magnificent array of thought leaders who serve as subject matter experts for *Futurescan 2020–2025: Health Care Trends and Implications.* The annual publication is designed to help leaders and professionals in the field negotiate the path ahead for some of the major factors creating transformation in health care.

The key theme this year is the need to simultaneously transition the core health care model while responding to the forces of disruption that threaten that model. More than 20 years ago, I wrote *The Second Curve: Managing the Velocity of Change* (Ballantine, 1996). The book had a simple premise: Most businesses in most industries were going along quite nicely on their "first curve" (their core business), where they made all their profit and revenue, but they had a sneaking suspicion that they could be threatened by a "second curve" (a new way of doing business) that would be radically different.

The drivers for the second curve were identified as demographic change, the rise of new consumers and technology (particularly the internet) and the growth of new markets in such countries as China and India. Operating on two curves is challenging, and a strategy must be developed that is robust enough to maximize the first curve while preparing for the second curve. As the book forecast, health care was relatively late to the second-curve party, whereas retail and financial services were already feeling the effects in the 1990s.

The articles in this year's *Futurescan* focus on some of these same drivers, as health care leaders confront the current wave of change.

Disruptive Innovation

As technology giants, mega retailers and others increasingly eye the health care sector as a growth opportunity, Aaron Martin, chief digital officer at Providence St. Joseph Health, says providers need to adapt to the new environment by implementing the following best practices:

- **Collaboration.** In areas where hospitals and health systems do not have a strong primary care presence, partnerships with retailers can help fill the gap through drugstore clinics and other options.
- **Innovation.** Some health systems are establishing their own retail-like operations and making care more convenient and accessible.

About the Author

Ian Morrison, Ph.D., is an author, consultant and futurist. He received an undergraduate degree from the University of Edinburgh, Scotland; a graduate degree from the University of Newcastle upon Tyne, England; and an interdisciplinary doctorate in urban studies from the University of British Columbia, Canada. He is the author of several books, including the bestselling *The Second Curve: Managing the Velocity of Change*. Morrison is the former president of the Institute for the Future and a founding partner of Strategic Health Perspectives, a forecasting service for clients in the health care industry.

- **Technology adoption.** In some instances, it may be highly desirable to adopt new technologies that hold promise for transforming health care in the future.
- **Preparation.** Whether health systems collaborate or choose to innovate on their own, they must get "transaction ready" to engage with consumers on a digital basis.

Dual Transformation

Robert W. Allen, FACHE, senior vice president and chief operating officer at Intermountain Healthcare, shares insights on how providers can disrupt the current environment and maintain incremental improvements and innovations at the same time.

According to Allen, four key challenges are driving the need for change: (1) financial pressures and the rising cost of care, (2) changing consumer expectations, (3) new entrants in the field and (4) empty hospital beds and underused facilities. Allen notes that leaders need to adapt their care delivery systems to current realities, while creating new health care platforms and sources of growth to thrive in the future. He says that strategies for success include preparing to transition from fee-for-service to value-based payment, becoming more consumer-centric and developing new care models and revenue streams for the future.

Strategic Partnerships

In the evolving landscape, health care leaders must seize the opportunity to form innovative partnerships that challenge the status quo as equally as they ensure the long-term relevance of their organizations, says Ninfa M. Saunders, D.H.A., FACHE, president and CEO of Navicent Health and an expert on the topic.

No longer is it strictly about health systems acquiring or merging with one another, as in the traditional partnerships of the past. Instead, the forces driving change are requiring them to identify new strategic alignments and redefine what success looks like. Rather than turning inward, many health systems are pursuing partnerships with other players, including retailers, technology firms, employers and local community organizations, to name a few. "Through partnerships, we can ensure we are creating healthy communities, addressing the needs of individuals and populations, and collaboratively creating a new focus on health that will be sustainable for years to come," concludes Saunders.

Resilience

Ronald A. Paulus, M.D., president and CEO of RAPMD Strategic Advisors and former president and CEO of Mission Health, says that "health care organizations are facing a critical need to find ways to build resilient workplaces." According to Paulus, leaders should prioritize keeping team members safe, reducing burnout, producing higher physician and employee satisfaction, and improving patient care.

"Executives can begin by engaging physicians and other team members in an open dialogue to identify key issues and pain points that need to be addressed," advises Paulus, who recommends that all stakeholders collaborate to develop an action plan for creating a culture that promotes organizational resilience. "When leaders take proactive steps . . . , the results can be game changing," he explains, emphasizing that "it is not only the right thing to do—it is good medicine."

Medical Advances

Today, medical advances are happening at an exponential rate and are reshaping the nation's health care system. "With the acceleration and convergence of a wide array of technologies, we have the ability to move beyond the current, reactive 'sick care'

model to one that is more continuous and preventive," says Daniel Kraft, M.D., chair for medicine at Singularity University and founder and chair of Exponential Medicine. He predicts the following key developments will transform the field over the next five years and beyond:

- Artificial intelligence.
- Wearables and quantified health.
- Genomic and precision medicine.
- Telehealth and virtual care.
- Virtual reality and augmented reality.

Kraft says the potential to proactively optimize health and wellness, detect disease at earlier stages and improve the treatment of acute and chronic conditions

---

Futurescan is designed to help leaders and professionals negotiate the path ahead for some of the key factors creating transformation in health care.

---

can become a reality if hospitals and health systems prioritize the implementation of these technologies.

Frictionless Health Care

Exploring strategies for removing friction from medical care is the focus of M. Bridget Duffy, M.D., chief medical officer of Vocera Communications. Duffy describes frictionless care as "a consistent, seamless experience of care from first impression to last where every person is treated with compassion and competence." She highlights several key action steps for health care leaders:

- Creating and embracing an organizational culture that values a human-centered approach to innovation.
- Concentrating on removing friction from care team communications and clinical workflows.
- Implementing technology that connects care teams and facilitates

the exchange of patient information in ways that are less burdensome to clinicians.

- Embracing the principles of patient- and family-centered care.

Duffy, one of the nation's leading experts on the patient and care team experience, says, "Health care leaders who partner with patients to establish a truly healing ecosystem will not only earn patient loyalty but also empower their clinicians to return to their true purpose: enabling people to heal."

Healthy Aging

Ken Dychtwald, Ph.D., founder of Age Wave and one of the foremost thought leaders on issues relating to aging, explains why the nation's medical system must adapt to the changing needs of older adults, who are increasingly technology savvy and wellness focused. He notes two parallel trends that are dramatically affecting the future of health care delivery for this population: the aging of the baby boomer generation and the growing number of elderly men and women who require intensive services. Identifying strategies to effectively address these trends—and the implications they hold for society overall—will

be a major challenge for hospitals and health systems over the next five years and beyond. Dychtwald proposes a five-part solution:

1. Use advances in medicine and technology to develop innovative solutions for healthy aging.
2. Promote research to reverse or cure Alzheimer's disease.
3. Find and recruit health care professionals specializing in gerontology.
4. Make lifelong disease prevention, management of chronic diseases and self-care national priorities.
5. Develop a humane approach to the end of life.

Medicaid

Andy Slavitt, former acting administrator for the Centers for Medicare & Medicaid Services, warns that Medicaid—which covers one in five Americans and accounts for nearly 20 percent of all U.S. personal health spending—is burdened by underfunding and is continually under political attack "despite the fact that it is, by any measure, a widely successful program."

Slavitt reviews state and federal efforts currently underway to reform

the program (e.g., Medicaid expansion, cost controls) and explores options for further potential solutions. He maintains that hospitals and health systems can play a key role in efforts to develop a sustainable model for Medicaid by collaborating with state governments in adopting innovative approaches, supporting efforts to transform the program and addressing social determinants of health. Health care leaders need "to step up and play an active and integral role in blazing the path forward for the Medicaid program," Slavitt concludes.

Conclusion

In an election year, all eyes are on politics and the uncertainties ahead. But some enduring trends will dominate the strategic agenda of hospitals and health systems no matter what the outcome. Disruptive innovation, dual transformation, strategic partnerships, organizational resilience, advances in medicine, frictionless care, healthy aging and Medicaid reform will be key challenges for the field in 2020 and beyond. *Futurescan 2020–2025* provides expert insights—informed by a survey of health care leaders from across the country—to light the way ahead.

Disruptive Innovation: The Impact of New Entrants on the Future of Health Care

with Aaron Martin

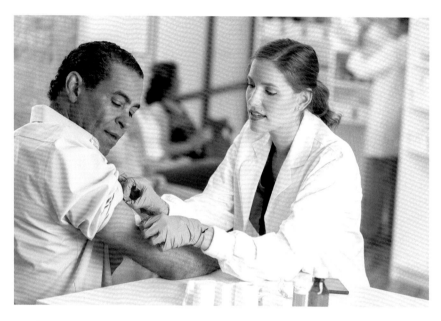

Health care executives may recall a time when "the competition" was another hospital across town. Much has changed since then, especially over the past year.

As major out-of-industry players enter the field with investments in infrastructure, technology, scientific research, and payment and delivery models, patients are increasingly finding more affordable and more accessible options that are transforming the nation's health care system. Moving forward, hospital and health system leaders will need to proactively respond to these disruptive innovations by adopting strategies that position their organizations to thrive in the evolving landscape.

Key Challenges Facing the Health Care Field

"The reasons technology giants such as Amazon, Google, and Apple and mega retailers CVS, Walgreens, Walmart and Best Buy are entering the health care space are numerous and compelling," says Aaron Martin, chief digital officer for Renton, Washington–based Providence St. Joseph Health (PSJH) and managing general partner at Providence Ventures, the health system's venture capital arm. These reasons include the following.

The size and scope of the medical field. According to the Centers for Medicare & Medicaid Services, health care spending in the United States reached a new high in 2018 of $3.65 trillion (Sisko et al. 2019). "Although our nation invests far more than any other country, the American health care system is inefficient, with room for improvements in access, care management and operations," notes Martin.

According to a study by the Commonwealth Fund, the United States ranked last among 11 highly developed countries for patient outcomes, health equity and quality of care, despite having the highest per capita health spending (Schneider et al. 2017). The study also found that poor access to primary care has led to insufficient control of chronic diseases and delayed diagnoses.

Many of the innovations being developed by the tech giants and mega retailers are addressing access to primary care and earlier diagnosis of health issues. For instance, in 2018, Google and Fitbit, the personal fitness tracker and wearables company,

About the Subject Matter Expert

Aaron Martin is chief digital officer at Providence St. Joseph Health based in Renton, Washington—the nation's third-largest health system—where he is responsible for digital innovation and marketing. He is also responsible for early-stage technology and medical device investments for Providence Ventures, a $300 million venture fund.

Martin serves on the boards of the Providence Ventures portfolio companies AVIA, Wildflower Health, Xealth and Kyruus. Prior to his role at Providence, he worked for Amazon and McKinsey and was an executive founder of two venture-backed technology companies.

FUTURESCAN SURVEY RESULTS
Disruptive Innovation

Health care executives from across the nation were asked how likely it is that the following will happen in their hospital or health system within the next five years.

By 2025, at least 15 percent of the outpatient services our hospital or health system delivers will be entirely digital/online.

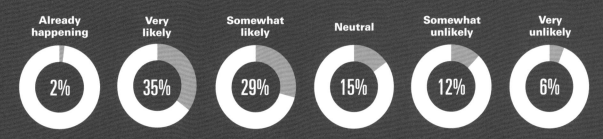

Already happening	Very likely	Somewhat likely	Neutral	Somewhat unlikely	Very unlikely
2%	35%	29%	15%	12%	6%

By 2025, our hospital or health system will have reduced its clinical space and increased the volume of digitally enabled care delivered outside the physical hospital setting.

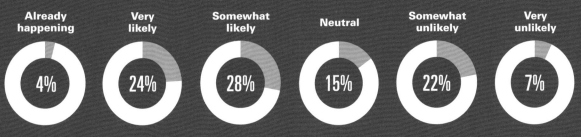

Already happening	Very likely	Somewhat likely	Neutral	Somewhat unlikely	Very unlikely
4%	24%	28%	15%	22%	7%

Note: Percentages may not sum exactly to 100 percent because of rounding.

---

announced a partnership that will enable Fitbit customers to link data from their devices with their electronic medical record using Google Cloud. The goal is to provide users with a greater awareness of their health and their physician with a better picture of their medical status.

The opportunity to engage an already loyal customer base. "While each of these mega corporations has its own business model, they all see entry into health care as another way to engage with and monetize their massive consumer base and serve their customers in new ways," says Martin. "This strategy also allows them to diversify their portfolios and bring their customer service expertise and new consumer technologies to a field that tends to lag behind in both arenas."

The tech giants are especially well positioned to help consumers find care more efficiently, according to Martin. Demand aggregators such as Amazon are becoming "digital front doors" that leverage artificial intelligence and voice assistant technology to facilitate health care interactions. For instance, in 2019 Amazon introduced new HIPAA (Health Insurance Portability and Accountability Act)–compliant Alexa capabilities that can help patients do the following:

- Connect with care via online scheduling.
- Check on home delivery of prescriptions.
- Manage health improvement goals.

More recently, Amazon announced Amazon Care, a telehealth and home-visit primary care offering for its employees. "Most industry experts believe this service will soon be made available to Amazon customers as well," says Martin.

The need to fill big-box floor space. Walmart, CVS, Best Buy and Walgreens are eyeing the field just as consumers are demanding greater retail-like access to and experiences with health care. The retailers are looking to fill their stores with profitable enterprises as floor space devoted to products diminishes as a result of increased online shopping.

"In-store primary care retail operations can bring profitable services in-house, create foot traffic and feed the pharmacy operation to compensate for the lost retail business moving online to Amazon," states Martin. For example, Walgreens teamed up with Microsoft in 2019 to create "digital health corners" and plans to invest $300 million in digital health (Garrity 2019). CVS Health announced plans in 2018 to spend between $325 million and $350 million on technology to offer more convenient health care options (Grant 2019). It also opened three Health-HUB locations in Texas. These storefronts offer services to help customers manage chronic conditions such as diabetes, hypertension and asthma. In addition to the pharmacy, each Health-HUB location has an expanded health clinic with a lab for blood testing and health screenings.

Implications for Health Care Leaders

Keeping up with these trends is vital to the future of hospitals and health systems. As patients assume more responsibility for medical costs and demand more convenient experiences, health care leaders have the opportunity to look outside their hospital for new ways to connect with patients more efficiently and effectively. "Commercially insured patients increasingly prefer digital care because of factors related to value, convenience and customer service," emphasizes Martin. "Quality is no longer a differentiator—it is assumed."

How likely is the field to adopt consumer-facing digital strategies? The latest *Futurescan* national survey of health care executives found that nearly two-thirds (64 percent) of respondents said it is somewhat to very likely that at least 15 percent of the outpatient services their organizations deliver will be entirely digital or online by 2025. In terms of reducing clinical space and increasing the volume of digitally enabled care delivered outside the hospital setting, there was less consensus; 52 percent of respondents believed it to be somewhat to very likely in the next five years.

To keep pace with this growing trend, Martin says leaders should consider the following strategies.

Collaboration. In areas where providers do not have a strong primary care presence, partnerships with retailers can help fill the gap through drugstore clinics and other options. "When these clinics need to refer patients with serious illnesses, conditions or diseases, hospitals and health systems should strive to be the destination of choice," advises Martin. This same principle applies to other health services that could be ripe for collaboration in a particular market. "It's important for leaders to create a rigorous, structured process to evaluate and identify the right partner. Each approach will be different, depending on the resources available," Martin says.

Innovation. Some forward-thinking health care organizations are innovating by establishing their own retail-like operations in the community, making their continuum of care more convenient and accessible and improving the customer experience. "The pace of change will soon go exponential, and providers need to be prepared to respond more quickly," emphasizes Martin. "They also should leverage the regional nature of their operation and trade best practices with their peers."

Technology adoption. In some instances, Martin says, it may be desirable to adopt promising new technologies, especially those focused on population health. These technologies include:

- Disease management using predictive analytics and wearables.
- Home-based health care technology and virtual visits with clinicians.
- Supply chain initiatives to improve the delivery of pharmaceuticals and medical equipment.

Preparation. Whether health care leaders collaborate or choose to innovate on their own, they must get "transaction ready" to engage with consumers on a digital basis. "This means building a

> What will differentiate providers in the future is the ability to offer personalized digital patient experiences.

consumer-facing digital platform—such as a smartphone app—to facilitate access, making it easier for patients to find the doctors and care they need, schedule appointments, set up telehealth visits, communicate with offices and pay bills online," says Martin. Once consumers engage with a provider digitally, he says, the provider should establish strong in-person and online relationships by enhancing personalization and tailoring content, products or services to specific audience segments.

Best Practices at Providence St. Joseph Health

Since joining PSJH in 2014, Martin has spearheaded the system's Digital Innovation Group, which is focused on creating online customer-centric care delivery models. The health system is currently involved in 17 ventures aimed at addressing some of the most difficult pain points in accessing health care. Two

such ventures are AVIA and Providence Express Care.

AVIA. This membership network of more than 40 health systems takes a strategic approach to collaboration to accelerate innovation and implement digital solutions that deliver positive financial and clinical results. "AVIA helps us select technology and evaluate the market to guide us in developing new technologies," says Martin.

Providence Express Care. For three years, PSJH has been enhancing access to its digital front door via platforms that enable consumers to engage with health system providers online. To link consumers with same-day primary care, Martin says, the digital team developed Express Care, a suite of medical services for patients needing nonemergent, low-acuity care. Consumers have three different Express Care options:

1. Express Care retail clinics offer walk-in visits.
2. Express Care Virtual links patients with a nurse practitioner via their smartphone, tablet or desktop computer.
3. Express Care at Home allows patients to schedule house calls from their digital device.

"Express Care was designed to be frictionless and deliver an online experience that's superior to in-person medical services," explains Martin. It features a customer service chatbot that uses artificial intelligence to direct patients to the appropriate point of care based on their symptoms, condition and answers to simple, frequently asked questions.

Express Care had almost 200,000 visits last year, of which 10 percent were telehealth and at-home visits. PSJH's low-acuity digital platform has made a significant impact on utilization, Martin says: By mid-2019, 30 percent of new in-clinic patient visits for Express Care were generated online, and the health system saw a 35 percent increase in new patient revenue. The platform has performed so well that the organization is spinning off the technology that powers Express Care into a separate company, DexCare, which will license it to other health systems. This will be the third company spin-off of technology created by the PSJH Digital Innovation Group—the first two being Xealth and Circle/Wildflower Health.

Best Practices at Other Organizations

Martin points to other best-practice examples in the health care field.

Wildflower Health. Wildflower Health has built a powerful personalization platform for integrating data, content and clinical resources delivered through smartphone-based technologies. The San Francisco–based company's white-label apps address the evolving needs of families, from family planning to pregnancy to pediatrics and beyond. The enterprise software allows providers to stay engaged with consumers, seamlessly integrating their resources to connect patients with health care services.

Wildflower Health's clients include health plans, providers and employers. In total, Wildflower's clients care for more than 50 million Americans. Since its inception, the company has grown from a pregnancy application into a digital solution that addresses evolving family health care needs. Providence incubated the provider-facing solution and sold it to Wildflower in 2018.

Inception Health. Milwaukee-based Froedtert & the Medical College of Wisconsin health network made a significant investment in digital health in 2015 when it established Inception Health. The organization was created to drive the adoption of digital health through collaboration with promising external innovators.

In the past four years, Inception Health has implemented more than 50 projects, most of which are live within the health system. They include the following:

- **Digital therapeutics for people with diabetes.** The service combines digital technology with a clinical team to help significantly lower A1c and keep it low.
- **Online cognitive behavioral therapy.** This program assists people in managing their depression, anxiety and stress on demand through a tool that empowers individuals but also connects them to their care team.
- **Artificial intelligence–powered symptom checker.** This service helps people better understand what may be ailing them and get connected with the most appropriate level of care to address their concern.

- **Digital maternity program.**
  Expectant women in the region
  can learn about and track their
  pregnancies at all stages at any time
  from their mobile device.
- **Digital medications.** People with
  a range of conditions are able
  to precisely see and share their
  medication ingestions with their
  care team by using a first-of-its-kind
  sensor-based system.
- **Digital care pathways.** People
  undergoing procedures at the health
  network are offered a tool that guides
  them through the process, checks
  in on them, and provides a way to
  connect with the care team seamlessly
  throughout the episode of care.

Conclusion

In today's environment, Martin says,
patients already assume that hospitals
and health systems provide high-quality
care. What will differentiate providers in
the future is the ability to offer personalized digital patient experiences. "Because
of the significant investments already
being made in health care by the tech
giants and retail corporations, conduct-
ing business as usual is not an option
for providers looking for long-term
viability," emphasizes Martin. "It will
be critical to meet consumers on their
terms, which—now more than ever—is
in the digital space where service, convenience and disruptive innovation are
paramount."

References

Garrity, M. 2019. "Walgreens to Invest $300M in Digital Health." *Becker's Hospital Review*. Published April 5. www.beckershospitalreview.com/healthcare-information-technology/walgreens-to-invest-300m-in-digital-health.html.

Grant, M. 2019. "CVS: Healthcare's Innovation Factory Is Just Down the Street." Adaptive Business Leaders Organization. Accessed December 10. https://roundtables.abl.org/cvs-healthcares-innovation-factory-just-down-street/.

Schneider, E.C., D.O. Sarnak, D. Squires, A. Shah and M.M. Doty. 2017. "Mirror, Mirror 2017: International Comparison Reflects Flaws and Opportunities for Better U.S. Health Care." Commonwealth Fund. Published July 14. www.commonwealthfund.org/publications/fund-reports/2017/jul/mirror-mirror-2017-international-comparison reflects-flaws-and.

Sisko, A.M., S.P. Keehan, J.A. Poisal, G.A. Cuckler, S.D. Smith, A.J. Madison, K.E. Rennie and J.C. Hardesty. 2019. "National Health Expenditure Projections, 2018–27: Economic and Demographic Trends Drive Spending and Enrollment Growth." *Health Affairs* 38 (3): 491–501.

Dual Transformation of Health Care: The Key to Sustainability

with Robert W. Allen, FACHE

With the steady transition to value-based payment models, hospitals and health systems need to consider a dual transformation strategy that adapts their care delivery systems to current realities while creating new health care platforms and sources of growth to thrive in the future.

Although the fee-for-service model is expensive and unsustainable, the adoption of value-based payment has been slow. Eventually, however, the vast majority of total health care payments will doubtless be based on outcomes and driven by cost efficiencies.

Dual Transformation in Health Care

"Dual transformation is critical for hospitals' short- and long-term sustainability," says Robert W. Allen, FACHE, senior vice president and chief operating officer at Intermountain Healthcare. The Utah-based health system has been creating innovative care delivery models for over a decade and is widely recognized as a leader in clinical quality improvement and efficient health care delivery. The system has won funding from the Centers for Medicare & Medicaid Services (CMS) as part of its Health Care Innovation Awards initiative.

According to Allen, the following challenges are driving the need to respond to the changing environment:

- **Financial pressures and the rising cost of care.** Health care expenditures are projected to grow 5.5 percent each year, on average, from 2018 to 2027 (Sisko et al. 2019). CMS continues to take the lead in linking payment to outcomes, and commercial payers are following suit. For instance, UnitedHealth Group announced in late 2018 that nearly half of its annual payments to providers—a total of $69 billion—are being made under its value-based care models (Japsen 2018).

- **Changing consumer expectations.** High-deductible health plans, which covered 25 percent of adults aged 18–64 who had employer-based health coverage in 2017 (Inserro 2018), are requiring employees to make more expensive health care purchasing decisions with price and convenience as key factors. In addition, the digitization of today's

About the Subject Matter Expert

Robert W. Allen, FACHE, Intermountain Healthcare's senior vice president and chief operating officer, was named one of the top 25 chief operating officers in health care by *Modern Healthcare* for the past two years. He has more than 25 years of health care executive leadership experience and has held administrator, CEO and vice president positions at hospitals and health organizations in Colorado, Wyoming, Utah, New Jersey and Massachusetts. In addition, Allen has served on many foundation, chamber and service boards. He is a Fellow of the American College of Healthcare Executives. He earned a bachelor's degree from Brigham Young University and a master of business administration degree from Utah State University.

FUTURESCAN SURVEY RESULTS
Dual Transformation

Health care executives from across the nation were asked how likely it is that the following will happen in their hospital or health system within the next five years.

By 2025, our hospital or health system will dedicate at least 15 percent of its business development funding to initiatives for entirely new sources of growth.

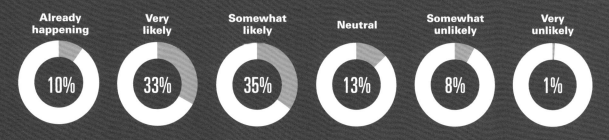

Already happening	Very likely	Somewhat likely	Neutral	Somewhat unlikely	Very unlikely
10%	33%	35%	13%	8%	1%

By 2025, our hospital or health system will have a dedicated function and funding specifically for transformational change.

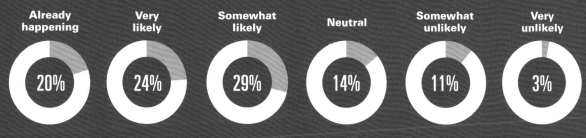

Already happening	Very likely	Somewhat likely	Neutral	Somewhat unlikely	Very unlikely
20%	24%	29%	14%	11%	3%

Note: Percentages may not sum exactly to 100 percent because of rounding.

consumer and heightened expectations generated by Amazon-level customer service are challenging hospitals and health systems to create new ways to enhance the patient experience.

- **New entrants in the health care arena.** With the United States home to the largest health care marketplace in the world, sizeable players such as Google, CVS, Walmart, Amazon and Apple, to name just a few, are beginning to attract new customers along the health care continuum in innovative ways, promising to be as disruptive as they are transformative.
- **Empty beds and underused facilities.** The gap between U.S. hospitals'

inpatient and outpatient revenue continued to shrink in 2017, the latest year for which data are available (American Hospital Association 2019). Hospitals' net outpatient revenue was $472 billion, or 95 percent of inpatient revenue, which totaled nearly $498 billion. As the shift from inpatient to outpatient care continues, hospitals will struggle with excess capacity and underused facilities.

Implications for Health Care Leaders

With these new realities, health care executives should consider how to strategically transition their hospitals to

new models of care and payment and adapt to changing consumer expectations. Allen notes that Intermountain Healthcare is prioritizing the development or expansion of access to points of care all along the continuum. "That is where the real opportunities are," he says. For example, Intermountain is piloting an initiative called Reimagined Primary Care, which takes a team-based approach to keeping its Medicare population well.

The initiative focuses on wellness visits, preventive screenings and telehealth to proactively help patients manage medications and chronic conditions. It also provides ready access to a nurse,

of services that we have established to help people receive care at the right time and place." More than a million lives in Intermountain's markets have health insurance that covers Connect Care.

Create new care models and revenue streams for the future. To achieve long-term sustainability, health care executives have the opportunity to be innovative and strategic in acquiring the technological capabilities and operational and service structures to thrive in the transformed future environment. From new care delivery models to novel revenue streams, forward-thinking health systems are already pioneering approaches to maintaining relevance and viability. Here are some examples:

in many cases outside of typical office hours. "By restructuring physician incentives around this initiative, we have found that the cost of care has gone down for patients in our pilot sites," Allen states. He adds that the initiative has about 31,000 patients enrolled and has seen impressive results, including a 35 percent decrease in emergency department admissions and a 60 percent decrease in hospital admissions.

Allen suggests that the following key principles can help hospital systems navigate the evolving health care landscape.

Prepare to transition from fee-for-service to value-based payment. Moving toward population health management with a refreshed focus on wellness requires new care models, investments in information technology and data management, increased efficiency and innovative payment methodologies. Hospitals and health systems may have to give up current margins for future positioning and prepare to accept risk in a variety of forms. Providers also will need to stay current and implement advances in medical technology and treatments that reduce costs and improve outcomes.

Become more consumer-centric. As new entrants appear in the health care marketplace, the stakes for winning patient

loyalty have never been higher. According to statistics released by Gallup in 2018, 75 percent of workers are satisfied with the quality of the health care they receive, but fewer (61 percent) are satisfied with the total cost they pay for that care. Nearly three-quarters of employed Americans (73 percent) say the health care system is "in a state of crisis" or "has major problems" (Reinhart 2018).

"With the growing desire for health care on demand, retail clinics and telemedicine providers are pulling patients away from traditional clinic settings," notes Allen. "To compete, hospitals must devise ways to serve patients the way they want, when and where they want it." Doing so may include providing digitally enabled care, such as telemedicine, or adopting a retail approach with convenient access points, consumer-centric amenities, convenient scheduling and easy bill paying.

Intermountain Healthcare has entered this space via Connect Care, which enables consumers to have video visits with clinicians 24 hours a day at a cost of $59 or less (depending on their insurance). "Eighty-one percent of Connect Care callers get their needs met over the phone," Allen says. "If we have to send a patient to a physician or to one of our InstaCare urgent care facilities for medical services, there is no charge for Connect Care. It is part of the continuum

- **Civica Rx.** A new, not-for-profit generic drug company, Civica Rx was established to help address the shortages and high prices of lifesaving medications. It was launched in 2018 by Intermountain Healthcare along with Catholic Health Initiatives, HCA Healthcare, Mayo Clinic, the Peterson Center on Healthcare, Providence St. Joseph Health, SSM Health and Trinity Health, among others. Civica Rx manufactured and distributed 14 hospital-administered generic drugs in 2019, with more to follow in 2020 and beyond. Civica Rx now includes more than a thousand hospital partners collaborating to produce generic medications and make them more widely available and affordable in medical centers across the nation.
- **Connect Care Pro.** Intermountain has expanded the concept of Connect Care to include medical professionals through Connect Care Pro, a virtual hospital. More than 40 services are provided via telemedicine, including neonatal resuscitation, behavioral health crisis support, intensive care unit (ICU) monitoring and antibiotic stewardship. Connect Care Pro brings high-level care to rural areas and at-risk populations, keeps patients in their communities and reduces the need for costly patient transfers. "It

helps fulfill Intermountain's ultimate goal of ensuring that patients get the right care, at the right time, and in the right place and that caregivers get the support they need to provide the best care for their patients," Allen says.

- **Mercy Virtual Care Center.** The world's first virtual care center opened in October 2015 with the goal of using telemedicine to help hospitals provide better care management for their patients. The four-story center in Chesterfield, Missouri, is the connected-care subsidiary of the multistate, 40-hospital Mercy network. It houses a large medical team that uses highly sensitive two-way cameras, online-enabled instruments and real-time vital signs monitoring to "see" patients wherever they are: in a bricks-and-mortar hospital, a physician's office or even the patient's home.

  The center offers a variety of services, including the largest single-hub electronic ICU in the nation; telehealth services to enhance stroke, pediatric and emergency care and to facilitate consultations between and among doctors, specialists and hospitalists; and the "vEngagement" program, which pairs care navigators with adults and children who have multiple chronic conditions.

- **Geisinger ProvenExperience.** Four years ago, Geisinger implemented ProvenExperience, a money-back guarantee that provides dissatisfied consumers with refunds for out-of-pocket costs such as co-pays, deductibles and coinsurance. For Geisinger, the program is a way to ensure that legitimate concerns do not recur in future consumer

interactions. Patient satisfaction scores have increased as a result, and the $997,806 that the health system has refunded between October 2015 and April 2018 is viewed as an investment in continuing to improve its scores over the long term. With CMS linking payment to patient satisfaction, ProvenExperience is also a way to help safeguard future Medicare revenue.

Conclusion

Dual transformation will be key to the future success of hospitals and health systems in 2020 and beyond. However, is the C-suite committed to it as an overarching strategy? The annual *Futurescan* survey asked executives across the country to share how far along they are in embracing some of the above-described concepts associated with dual transformation. The results indicate that 10 percent of respondents already dedicate at least 15 percent of business devel-

opment funding to initiatives for entirely new sources of growth, while 68 percent think it somewhat to very likely they will seek out new sources of growth by 2025. "Clearly, the need to diversify beyond traditional revenue streams is on the radar scope of most health care executives," Allen says.

In addition, in terms of hospitals or health systems having a dedicated function and funding specifically for transformational change, the "already happening" percentage doubled to 20 percent. The survey findings thus show that the vast majority of executives have dual transformation on their agendas.

"It is exciting to see ever more diverse approaches unfold to address the issues that are challenging us in health care," Allen says. "Taken together, these innovations are helping to create a future where patients are truly at the center of the health care ecosystem. It is simply the right thing to do."

References

American Hospital Association. 2019. *2019 AHA Hospital Statistics.* Chicago: American Hospital Association.

Inserro, A. 2018. "Enrollment in High-Deductible Health Plans Continues to Grow." *American Journal of Managed Care.* Published August 9. www.ajmc.com/newsroom/enrollment-in-highdeductible-health-plans-continues-to-grow.

Japsen, B. 2018. "UnitedHealth Group's Value-Based Care Spend Hits $69 Billion." *Forbes*. Published October 17. www.forbes.com/sites/brucejapsen/2018/10/17/unitedhealth-groups-value-based-care-spend-hits-69-billion/.

Reinhart, R.J. 2018. "In the News: Americans' Satisfaction with Their Healthcare." Gallup. Published February 2. https://news.gallup.com/poll/226607/news-americans-satisfaction-healthcare.aspx.

Sisko, A.M., S.P. Keehan, J.A. Poisal, G.A. Cuckler, S.D. Smith, A.J. Madison, K.E. Rennie and J.C. Hardesty. 2019. "National Health Expenditure Projections, 2018–27: Economic and Demographic Trends Drive Spending and Enrollment Growth." *Health Affairs* 38 (3): 491–501.

The Changing Face of Strategic Health Care Partnerships

with Ninfa M. Saunders, D.H.A., FACHE

The world of strategic partnerships in health care is undergoing a sea change. No longer is it strictly about health systems acquiring or merging with one another, as in the traditional partnerships of the past. Indeed, the number of hospital mergers and acquisitions has been on the decline since 2015; 95 deals were recorded that year, compared to just 67 deals in 2018 (Daly 2019).

Instead, emerging and evolving types of partnerships are challenging health care leaders to respond quickly, identify new strategic alignments and redefine what success looks like. Rather than turning inward, many health systems are pursuing impactful and strategic collaborations with fellow providers and other types of organizations as they adjust to the transformation of the field.

The Driving Forces of Change

"What got us here will not get us there" is an oft-quoted maxim used to motivate leaders to actively consider new and innovative ways to address the challenges health care faces. "Our industry is being inundated with forces that demand urgent change, and we are

compelled to act quickly to ensure our long-term sustainability and relevance," says Ninfa M. Saunders, D.H.A., FACHE, president and CEO of Navicent Health, an Atrium Health system. For example:

- Timely and appropriate access to care remains an obstacle.
- The ever-escalating and unsustainable cost of care continues to affect every part of the health care ecosystem.

- Inequity and disparity in care processes and outcomes persist despite many efforts focused on patient-centered care.
- Care modalities and access points are being replaced by new technologies enabled by the acceleration of a digital front-door strategy.
- An increasing focus on value is demanding more sustainable, outcomes-based solutions and

About the Subject Matter Expert

Ninfa M. Saunders, D.H.A., FACHE, is president and CEO of Navicent Health, an Atrium Health system headquartered in Georgia that consists of more than 1,000 licensed beds at over 30 locations for medical, surgical, rehabilitation and hospice care. Saunders has a wealth of hospital administration and clinical experience. A co-founder of the Stratus Healthcare network in Georgia, she currently serves on the board of the Georgia Hospital Association and as chair of the Georgia Alliance of Community Hospitals.

Previously, she served as chair of the American Hospital Association's Institute for Diversity and Health Equity. Recognized as a national thought leader in health care, Saunders is a member of the editorial board of *Healthcare Transformation* and has contributed articles to a number of health care publications. She also has been a frequent expert panelist in health care roundtables and forums and serves on the President's Leadership Council of Thomas Jefferson University and Health System.

FUTURESCAN SURVEY RESULTS
Strategic Partnerships

Health care executives from across the nation were asked how likely it is that the following will happen in their hospital or health system within the next five years.

By 2025, our hospital or health system will have at least three vertical partnerships (i.e., partnerships with organizations within its supply chain, such as payers, insurers, and pharmaceutical suppliers).

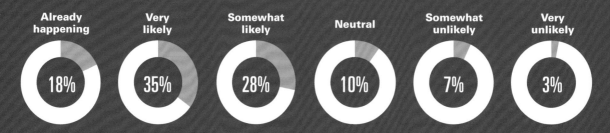

Already happening	Very likely	Somewhat likely	Neutral	Somewhat unlikely	Very unlikely
18%	35%	28%	10%	7%	3%

By 2025, our hospital or health system will base its growth strategy more on partnerships, mergers or acquisitions than on direct patient recruitment.

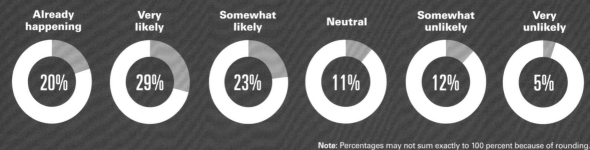

Already happening	Very likely	Somewhat likely	Neutral	Somewhat unlikely	Very unlikely
20%	29%	23%	11%	12%	5%

Note: Percentages may not sum exactly to 100 percent because of rounding.

requiring health care providers to accommodate a commoditized pricing approach.

- A shift from diagnostic encounters to episodic care management is driving a population health approach instead of a focus on the health of individuals.
- Consumerism grounded in meeting the needs of a multigenerational market has become a reality.
- Disruption and innovation in health care are being accelerated by new and nontraditional market entrants.
- The technology and retail sectors are compelling health care to engage with consumers in different and convenient

ways, including through use of self-monitoring devices that capture meaningful lifestyle data that can be correlated to clinical and wellness needs.

Traditional and Current Partnerships

Fortunately, many health systems have been able to pivot quickly in the new environment by collaborating with a variety of other organizations and taking on more risk.

The latest national *Futurescan* survey of health care executives found that 18 percent of respondents already have entered into at least three vertical

partnerships with organizations in their supply chain, and another 63 percent are somewhat or very likely to do so within the next five years. In addition, 72 percent of respondents said their growth strategy either already is based more on partnerships, mergers or acquisitions than on direct patient acquisition or is somewhat to very likely to be by 2025.

The American Hospital Association has identified several types of strategic partnerships that have successfully moved beyond the traditional mergers and acquisitions of the past (Allen et al. 2016). These arrangements include the following (further detailed in exhibit 1):

- Mergers for population health management.
- New companies.
- Joint ventures.
- Management services agreements.
- Brand/expertise extensions.

"In evaluating the success of strategic partnerships, partners often share the same primary objective: accretion for each other," notes Saunders. In other words, each partner gains value through one or more of the following core economies in McKinsey's value proposition model for mergers and acquisitions (Malani, Sherwood and Sutaria 2013):

- **Economies of scale** gained through efficiency and productivity-driven measures.
- **Economies of scope** created through the codevelopment and cofunding of new initiatives.
- **Economies of structure** achieved through the elimination of duplicative functional departments or services.
- **Economies of skill** gained through the mining, retention and sharing of clinical and administrative talent.

"These economies have proved time and time again to be vital outcomes of traditional partnerships," says Saunders. "They are just as critical to the new and novel partnership models that more and more health care providers are pursuing as they seek near- and long-term success."

Emerging and Innovation-Based Partnerships

Other nontraditional and innovative partnership models are becoming increasingly essential to health care organizations as they address the broad challenges in the industry, according to Saunders. The continuum of options is expansive (and still expanding) and includes the following, among many others:

Exhibit 1

Types of Strategic Partnerships

Model	Description	Example
Merger for population health management	Merging/partnering to provide the larger geographic reach required to be successful in population health management.	**Geisinger Health System and AtlantiCare.** Rather than purchasing AtlantiCare, Geisinger developed a 10-year commitment with the New Jersey–based health system that makes it Geisinger's foundational partner in New Jersey. Mutual agreements are required for any strategic initiatives in the southern part of the state, and overall collaboration is undertaken for initiatives in the rest of the state and Philadelphia.
New company	Joining together of two health care organizations to create an entirely new company.	**Beaumont Health.** This Michigan health system was created through the merger of three health systems in the greater Detroit area.
Joint venture	Short- or long-term arrangement between a hospital or health system and other entities offering entirely unrelated products.	**Vivity.** This narrow-network health plan was a joint venture between Anthem Blue Cross and seven health systems in Southern California, all of which share risk.
Management services agreement	A fee-based contractual arrangement in which a larger health system provides partial or full management services to a smaller organization.	**Novant Health Shared Services.** This entity offers a variety of products to community hospitals, including management of supply chain/purchasing, revenue cycle, clinical equipment and service lines.
Brand/expertise extension	Using a well-known health care brand to increase visibility and offer new services.	**Mayo Clinic Care Network.** Providers can join this network after a comprehensive evaluation process, then share Mayo's branding and expertise while still retaining autonomy.

Source: Allen et al. (2016).

HEALTH CARE TRENDS AND IMPLICATIONS **17**

- Hospitals and health systems collaborating with local organizations to address public health issues and social determinants of health.
- Partnerships with retailers and technology firms to develop innovative health offerings.
- Direct contracting with employers to provide medical services to their employees.
- Start-ups that leverage new solutions to improve patient care.
- Multiple hospitals and health systems forming a network of "problem solvers" to collectively address targeted health or payment issues.
- The formation of new companies (led sometimes by traditional health systems, sometimes by disruptive new entrants) that are designing new models of health care delivery, access and wellness.

Each hospital or health system should evaluate these models carefully to determine the approach and structure that are best suited to its needs, says Saunders. Most will pursue a plurality of models, as Navicent Health, a leading health system based in central Georgia, recently did (see sidebar).

"To drive success, Navicent Health sets specific goals for its strategic partnerships and ensures that each aligns with the organization's mission and core value proposition," explains Saunders. In addition, each partnership must support the organization's enterprise strategic plan and at least one of its four guiding strategic objectives: (1) engage consumers/patients in meaningful ways, (2) create healthy communities, (3) demonstrate value by taking on risk and (4) leverage disruptive technologies effectively.

Saunders says that "Navicent Health has worked hard to evolve the understanding of these relationships. Although some were viewed in the past as mere vendors, they are in fact partners in the truest sense of the word." Navicent Health knows the organization must not become distracted by the "shiny object" nature of new technology (e.g., artificial intelligence, wearables, sensors) and realizes its relationships with technology partners are addressing a fundamental process.

As Navicent Health's chief strategy officer/chief innovation officer points out, "while the creation of new and refined technologies is certainly needed, it is just as important to understand the importance of addressing the underlying process or model and not just the technology. If you place a new technology over a dysfunctional process or model . . . you'll likely still have a dysfunctional process or model that hasn't been addressed. Organizations need a balance between the technologies and the underlying models or processes for optimal creation of change to be achieved" (Cornue 2018). For this reason, the health system focuses on processes and systems in its partnerships

Navicent Health's Partnership Models

Navicent Health has been at the forefront of developing nontraditional partnerships with start-ups and establishing companies in the health care space. Often these partnerships address huge challenges faced by Navicent Health's service areas, such as community health, disparities, access to care, resources and distributed care. Their success is measured by impactful outcomes that are critical to the future success of any health care organization: decreased costs, new revenue streams, elimination of disparities, opportunities to connect with patients and consumer loyalty, among others.

Horizontal Partnerships

Stratus Healthcare. Stratus Healthcare is a nonequity collaborative involving multiple hospitals throughout central and southern Georgia. The partnership's focus is to use scale, scope and structure to address potential clinical gaps in services and technology while collectively developing strategies that support these regional hospitals as they serve their local communities.

Atrium Health. Navicent Health joined the Atrium Health network as part of a strategic combination that allows Atrium Health to ensure health equity, access and affordability by addressing the needs of patients and communities across a larger area of the Southeast. For example, the partnership enables Atrium Health to expand its telehealth network into Georgia and provide telehealth access to Navicent Health patients in rural and underserved areas. This partnership is achieving other economies of scale, scope, structure and skill, including leveraging best practices and processes; expanding on innovative efforts to drive change; complementing key service line strategies; and advancing a culture focused on teammates, key partners and care for all.

Australia's Commonwealth Scientific and Industrial Research Organisation (CSIRO). Along with health system partners such as Queensland Hospital, CSIRO established this partnership to promote collaboration among local clinicians and world-class scientists on significant issues in

(continued)

(continued from previous page)

rural health and health disparities—for example, adapting CSIRO's technology to assist clinicians in digital management of high-risk pregnancies in underserved populations.

Vertical Partnerships

SynsorMed. A digital health platform company, SynsorMed came to Navicent Health as an early-stage start-up to embed its technical team with Navicent Health's respiratory therapists and community workers. Its sole focus is to close health disparity gaps in populations of patients with chronic obstructive pulmonary disease.

Clean Hands, Safe Hands. In this partnership, an early-stage product company worked with a select group of nurses and experts in Navicent Health's quality department to accelerate the pace of new hand hygiene protocols. Navicent Health's providers are empowered to work at the top of their licenses while having a partner that is both nimble in its approach to problem solving and motivated to ensure its solutions are aligned with clinical standards.

Hybrid Partnerships

Advanced Technology Development Center (ATDC). ATDC at the Georgia Institute of Technology has been Georgia's technology incubator since 1980. In 2018 it launched its HealthTech Program, with Navicent Health as the founding health system partner. One company incubated at ATDC, Corstrata, helps address Georgia's statewide nurse shortage by offering virtual support to one of Navicent Health's post-acute care facilities, managing complex wounds without the need for hiring additional certified wound care nurses.

Cox Communication. Cox Communication is a subsidiary of Cox Enterprises, a privately held global company headquartered in Georgia with a strong commitment to the health and well-being of its employees and customers. This partnership demonstrates how private–public partnerships can extend beyond philanthropy into codeveloped solutions for health care systems, enabling clinically acceptable products to support home care and redefining the clinical algorithm of care with appropriate data insights.

and ensures that technology is working to solve a bigger problem or is a tool for a larger process.

Conclusion

Looking ahead, the typical health care "partnership" will clearly continue to evolve in newer and more impactful ways as the U.S. delivery system navigates the uncertainty of the 2020s. The ability to get comfortable with the unknown is a leadership skill set that will be challenged over and over again.

"The reality of the next 10 years is that we need to reinvent the legacy health care system and accept that impending obsolescence is forcing us to reconsider our current orientation," says Saunders. To this end, speed and execution will be not only important differentiators but also likely the only way hospitals and health systems can achieve the transformation needed for future success.

Saunders advises leaders to seize the opportunity to create new, innovative and impactful partnerships that

challenge the status quo as equally as they ensure the longer-term relevance of their organizations. "Partnerships may be the only way we can successfully disrupt a health care system that is in dire need of change," she emphasizes. "Through partnerships, we can ensure we are creating healthy communities, addressing the needs of individuals and populations, and collaboratively creating a new focus on health that will be sustainable for years to come. What better charge is there in the work we are doing than that?"

References

Allen, P.M., M.J. Finnerty, R.S. Gish, M.E. Grube, K.A. Kamholz, A.R. Singh, J.P. Smyth and R.W. York. 2016. *Guide to Health Care Partnerships for Population Health Management and Value-Based Care*. Hospitals in Pursuit of Excellence. Published July. www.hpoe.org/Reports-HPOE/2016/guide-to-health-care-partnerships-pop-health.pdf.

Cornue, C. 2018. "Disruption and Innovation as a Means to Create Change in Healthcare." *Atlanta Business Chronicle*. Published October 29. www.bizjournals.com/atlanta/news/2018/10/29/viewpoint-disruption-and-innovation-as-a-means-to.html.

Daly, R. 2019. "Hospital M&A Deals Slow in 2018." Healthcare Financial Management Association. Published January 14. www.hfma.org/topics/news/2019/01/62793.html.

Malani, R., A. Sherwood and S. Sutaria. 2013. "The Smarter Scale Equation." McKinsey & Company. Published May. https://healthcare.mckinsey.com/sites/default/files/793545_The_Smarter_Scale_Equation.pdf.

Building a Resilient Health Care Organization

with Ronald A. Paulus, M.D.

I t may seem like an oversimplification, but hospitals and health systems are first and foremost in the people business. The mission of healing patients and relieving their suffering relies on compassionate, highly trained professionals who work effectively in teams to deliver health care services that improve lives.

A reasonable assumption is that high-functioning teams deliver the best medical outcomes and best overall patient experience. So what happens when team members themselves are experiencing stressors so severe that they affect their mental health; their relationships with patients, coworkers and family; and their quality of life?

"Unfortunately, too many health care organizations are finding out how burnout, compassion fatigue and a fear of workplace violence are affecting the caregivers that patients depend on to care for them," says Ronald A. Paulus, M.D., president and CEO of RAPMD Strategic Advisors and former president and CEO of Mission Health in Asheville, North Carolina. "In a system that has grown increasingly complex, health care organizations are facing a critical need to find ways to

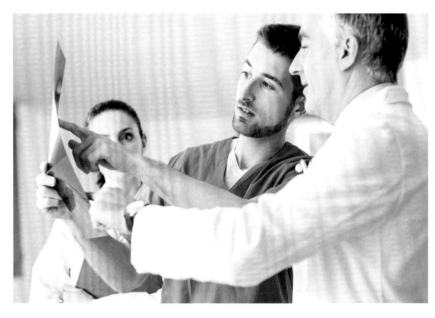

build resilient workplaces that keep team members safe, reduce burnout, produce higher physician and employee satisfaction, and improve the patient experience."

Key Challenges Facing the Health Care Field

For many years, stress and burnout have been growing among physicians and nurses on the front lines of patient care, as well as among other hospital and health system workers. Although one contributing factor has been the difficulty in documenting the problem, a growing number of studies quantifying the extent of burnout are helping to bring the issue to light. According to a Medscape report (Kane 2019), nearly half of U.S. physicians are experiencing burnout, as are their nursing colleagues (Brown, Whichello and Price 2018) and other members of the care team.

About the Subject Matter Expert

Ronald A. Paulus, M.D., is president and CEO of RAPMD Strategic Advisors, a health care advisory company serving health systems and health technology companies. He is immediate past president and CEO of Mission Health, a $2 billion integrated health system serving western North Carolina. Under his leadership, Mission Health became the only health system ever designated by IBM Watson Health as one of the 15 Top Health Systems in six of seven years. Before joining Mission Health, Paulus led clinical operations and innovation for Geisinger

Health. Prior to that, he was co-founder and president of CareScience, a quality/efficiency analytics platform used by nearly 1,000 hospitals nationwide. Paulus received his M.D., M.B.A. and B.S. degrees from the University of Pennsylvania. He has frequently published peer-reviewed journal articles and speaks regularly on health care quality, innovation, leadership and new care models. He has been named several times to *Modern Healthcare*'s list of the Top 50 Most Influential Physician Executives and Leaders.

FUTURESCAN SURVEY RESULTS
Resilience

Health care executives from across the nation were asked how likely it is that the following will happen in their hospital or health system within the next five years.

By 2025, one of the top three threats to our hospital's or health system's clinical outcomes will be workforce burnout and a lack of resilience.

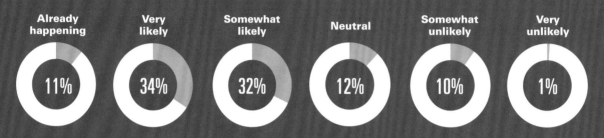

Already happening	Very likely	Somewhat likely	Neutral	Somewhat unlikely	Very unlikely
11%	34%	32%	12%	10%	1%

By 2025, our hospital or health system will achieve better clinical outcomes by building a more resilient health care workforce.

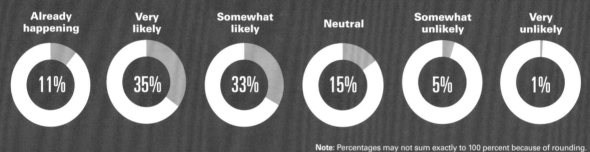

Already happening	Very likely	Somewhat likely	Neutral	Somewhat unlikely	Very unlikely
11%	35%	33%	15%	5%	1%

Note: Percentages may not sum exactly to 100 percent because of rounding.

"Burnout manifests itself in a variety of ways, ranging from increased stress to mental health and physical health issues, to compassion fatigue, to concern for personal safety, to alcohol and substance abuse, to a greater risk for suicide," says Paulus.

Major causes of burnout among clinicians include the following:

- The increase in violence and other threats to the safety of physicians, nurses and allied health professionals in the workplace, sometimes the result of a hostile environment.
- A workload that has grown exponentially because of the mandated use of electronic health records (EHRs) and government and health insurer documentation requirements, which reduce the amount of time physicians and nurses can spend on direct patient care.
- Less time to spend with family and to connect with other health care professionals because of work demands.
- Economic and reimbursement factors that put pressure on health systems to reduce costs and staffing levels, requiring the remaining clinicians to do more with less.

Across the health care continuum, Paulus says, the impact of burnout is having detrimental effects on patient care and workplace stability. The results of this year's national *Futurescan* survey of health care executives further validate the extent of the problem: 77 percent of respondents indicated that workforce burnout and a lack of resilience either already are among the top three threats to the clinical outcomes of hospitals and health systems or will be by 2025. The phenomenon manifests itself in several ways, including the following:

- Increased medical errors and patient safety events caused by clinician fatigue.

- Decreased physician and employee productivity.
- Higher rates of attrition and turnover among physicians, nurses and other workers, which create significant staffing challenges and drive up recruitment costs.
- Diminished clinician capacity to show empathy to patients.
- Decreased patient satisfaction.

Clearly, burnout and a lack of resilience are critical issues that need to be addressed for the sake of clinicians and patients alike.

Implications for Health Care Leaders

"It is fundamentally important that senior hospital and health system leaders acknowledge clinician and health care worker safety and burnout as significant problems and make an organization-wide commitment to solving these challenges," states Paulus. "Executives can begin by engaging physicians and other team members in an open dialogue to identify key issues and pain points that need to be addressed." He recommends that all stakeholders work together to develop an action plan supported by a dedicated budget for creating a sustainable culture and infrastructure that promote resilience and well-being. The action plan should accomplish the following:

- Keep physicians and other team members safe in the work environment by teaching de-escalation skills, establishing behavioral emergency response teams and providing staff with a discreet method for notifying others that they need help when they find themselves in a potentially violent situation.
- Give physicians and nurses a voice in organizational decisions that directly affect them, and give them more control over their environment.
- Help clinicians reconnect with their purpose and their calling in patient care to restore joy in work.
- Ensure that communication between team members is polite, respectful and focused on active listening.

- Find ways to streamline physicians' and nurses' administrative and documentation tasks, workloads and workflows.
- Provide resilience education, coaching and support, and offer wellness and mental health services to caregivers and other workers.
- Implement reward and recognition programs designed to highlight the many successes that occur daily but are too often taken for granted.

Because these problems span all hospitals and health systems regardless of size, setting and scope of service, Paulus says, the crisis of clinician safety and burnout is attracting the attention of concerned health care leaders across the country. Discussions on burnout are now prompting some organizations to advocate for a "Quadruple Aim" that builds on the Institute for Healthcare Improvement's Triple Aim by adding clinician satisfaction to the goals of improving the health of populations, enhancing the experience of care for individuals, and reducing the cost of health care.

The Institute for Healthcare Excellence, in partnership with the American Hospital Association and Vocera, is supporting the National Taskforce for Humanity in Healthcare (NTH) in implementing a pilot program in five health systems across the country.

The NTH pilot is a multistep, comprehensive initiative aimed at reducing physician burnout, instilling joy and purpose in daily work, and enhancing the performance of individuals, teams and care delivery organizations. WakeMed, a 941-bed hospital system in North Carolina, is one of the pilot sites rolling out the NTH program in several primary care and urology clinics. "We are doing this work to promote a positive work culture, to support staff and provider retention, and most importantly, to ensure that our patients receive the health care experience they deserve," says Theresa Amerson, M.D., a local leader who helped guide the pilot program. "This is what everyone needs."

Across the country, other initiatives are starting to show promising results in improving team communications, physician and employee satisfaction, and resilience skills. Following are some examples.

Reducing hassles in the work environment. HCA Healthcare comprises 180 hospitals and 2,000 sites of care. HCA had three different EHRs with variation in documentation content, which nursing staff cited as a leading pain point in engagement surveys. To address the issue, a new program, Evidence-Based Clinical Documentation (EBCD), was developed by small teams of practicing nurses based on an ideal workflow. EBCD ensured that documentation was meaningful for patient care or necessary for billing or regulatory requirements. In addition, mobile monitors were deployed that automated the entry of patient vital signs by uploading them directly into the EHR. EBCD was piloted and refined at one hospital and then extended to nine additional hospitals. The new documentation program resulted in a time savings of 45 minutes per 12-hour nursing shift, and automation of vital sign data entry saved an additional 30 minutes per shift while shortening the time to view "real-time" vital signs from 41 minutes to 23 seconds. The new program has effectively addressed one of nursing's primary pain points and is currently used in 172 hospitals within the system.

> When leaders take proactive steps to ensure a safer and more productive work environment, the results can be game changing.

Ensuring effective, polite and active listening–based communication among all team members. Mission Health in North Carolina has made great strides in quality improvement, cost reductions and patient satisfaction. However, its employee engagement scores (the percentage of team members who are actively engaged) lagged behind the national average of 18.5 percent. In 2018, Mission Health piloted a program consisting of brief, weekly one-on-one online communications between managers and their team members. During each exchange, employees tell their managers what they will need from them that week, as well as what they loved and loathed about their work during the preceding week. Employees also rate the value that they contributed and how often they were able to work in their core strengths. Within less than a

year of implementing the program, Mission Health's percentage of fully engaged employees rose to 34 percent, showing a marked improvement in job satisfaction.

Ensuring that all staff members are safe in the work environment. Although fewer than 33 percent of nurses report incidents of violence experienced on the job, 25 percent report being physically assaulted and 60 percent report being bullied (Joint Commission 2018). The problem is so concerning that the Joint Commission issued a sentinel event alert on workplace violence in April 2018. To address the issue, Thomas Jefferson University Hospital in Philadelphia partnered with Strongline to develop Bluetooth-activated alert badges for patient-facing staff members. When threatened, a staff member can press a button on the badge to notify security and nearby team members, who can immediately engage to help de-escalate the situation. The alert includes the name of the staff member and his or her current, real-time location.

Building the resilience of team members. Novant Health in Winston-Salem, North Carolina, developed a personal leadership development program to foster discussion about well-being, resilience and stress reduction among physicians and other health care professionals. Championed and facilitated by Tom Jenike, M.D., a family physician and the system's chief human experience officer, the Novant Health Leadership Development Program enables participants to reconnect with the reasons they chose medicine, establish personal and professional priorities, and build a sustainable model

of resilience and well-being to enhance performance in their personal and professional lives. The program, which offers continuing medical education and continuing nursing education credits, has more than 2,000 graduates and hosts quarterly alumni retreats to promote sustainability. Currently, program participants rank in the 97th percentile for employee engagement and alignment and have become catalysts for system changes to support a culture of organizational resilience and well-being.

Focusing on personal resilience. Implementation of Life Cross Training (Life XT), a human performance program based on evidence-based techniques to enhance personal wellness and resilience, has been well received at Mission Health. The initial pilot included 50 participants from Mission Health's executive team; medical staff; and nursing, administrative and support areas. During a four-month period, they were exposed to wellness and resilience techniques such as meditation, gratitude and reflection. Upon completion of the pilot, 93 percent agreed the training had helped them with focus and productivity, 94 percent said it helped them to know when they needed to take care of themselves, and 97 percent stated they would recommend it to others.

Conclusion

The foregoing examples from leading health systems accord with Paulus' view that "the good news is the vast majority of health system executives across the country are beginning to recognize burnout as a systemic problem and are starting to commit to addressing its causes."

This perspective is further underscored by the *Futurescan* survey, which found that nearly eight in ten leaders (79 percent) say their hospital or health care system either has achieved better clinical outcomes through building a more resilient health care workforce or is somewhat to very likely to do so by 2025.

Crucial to the success of these efforts, according to Paulus, is developing an organizational culture that fosters resilience at every level of the health care system. "When leaders take pro-active steps to ensure a safer and more productive work environment, listen to their workforce, explore ways to address burnout, and help clinicians and other health care employees reconnect with the reasons they chose health care as a profession, the results can be game changing."

Benefits to hospitals and health systems include increased physician, nurse and employee satisfaction; improved clinical outcomes; and higher patient satisfaction. "It is not only the right thing to do—it is good medicine," emphasizes Paulus.

References

Brown, S., R. Whichello and S. Price. 2018. "The Impact of Resiliency on Nurse Burnout: An Integrative Literature Review." *MedSurg Nursing* 27 (6): 349–78.

Joint Commission. 2018. "Physical and Verbal Violence Against Health Care Workers." *Sentinel Event Alert* 59. Published April 17. www.jointcommission.org/assets/1/18/SEA_59_Workplace_violence_4_13_18_FINAL.pdf.

Kane, L. 2019. "Medscape National Physician Burnout, Depression & Suicide Report 2019." Medscape. Published January 19. www.medscape.com/slideshow/2019-lifestyle-burnout-depression-6011056.

Technologies That Are Shaping the Future of Health and Medicine

with Daniel Kraft, M.D.

Health care innovation is moving at a faster pace than at any time in history, driving toward a model of connected, data-driven and more personalized care. From artificial intelligence (AI) to genomics, wearables and more, medical advances are happening at an exponential rate and are reshaping our delivery system.

"With the acceleration and convergence of a wide array of technologies, we have the ability to move beyond the current, reactive 'sick care' model to one that is more continuous and preventive," says Daniel Kraft, M.D., chair for medicine at Singularity University and founder and chair of Exponential Medicine. "The potential to proactively optimize health and wellness, detect and prevent disease at earlier stages, and better treat acute and chronic conditions can become a reality if hospital and health system leaders leverage these solutions to help transform care."

Kraft predicts that several key developments will transform health care as we know it over the next five years and beyond.

Artificial Intelligence

AI is advancing medicine through numerous applications in such specialties as radiology, pathology, dermatology and surgery, where it is greatly enhancing diagnostic capabilities and the selection of therapies to improve patient access and outcomes, according to Kraft. For instance, the use of AI accelerates the detection of problem areas on tests ranging from standard chest X-rays to computed tomography (CT) and ultrasound scans. More recently, the technology has been used in colonoscopies to identify potentially cancerous polyps and to help physicians make more expedient diagnoses and deliver increasingly precise treatments.

Kraft points out that the use of AI in health care may also help mitigate burnout among physicians by reducing their cognitive workload, quickly

About the Subject Matter Expert

Daniel Kraft, M.D., is a Stanford- and Harvard-trained physician-scientist, inventor, entrepreneur and innovator. With more than 25 years of experience in clinical practice, biomedical research and health care innovation, he has served as faculty chair for medicine at Singularity University since its inception, and as the founder and chair of Exponential Medicine, a program that explores convergent, rapidly developing technologies and their potential in biomedicine and health care. Kraft is a graduate of Brown University and Stanford Medical School and completed his residency at Massachusetts General Hospital. He founded RegenMed Systems; has multiple digital health, medical device, immunology and stem cell–related patents; and served on the faculty at Stanford and the University of California, San Francisco. He is an Aspen Institute Health Innovator Fellow and a Kauffman Fellow.

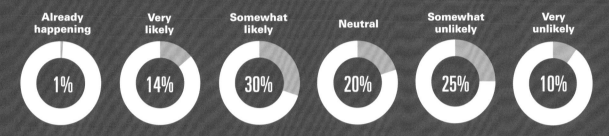
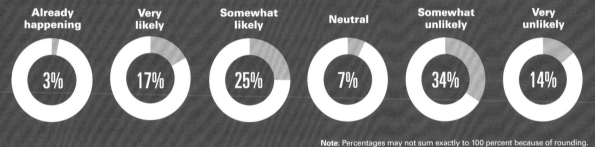
mining copious amounts of patient data in electronic medical records (EMRs) and automating some of the documentation required by payers. AI is also enabling health systems to unlock the potential of large scientific and patient databases for use in predictive analytics and to improve clinical care and lower costs.

Clinicians and data scientists at Brigham and Women's Hospital in Boston have used AI in integrated clinical, experimental and machine learning approaches to predict and prevent infections. For example, these models are defining how microbiota in the digestive system prevent patients from acquiring or developing active infections with *C. difficile*, the most common hospital-acquired bacterium in the United States.

Considerations for providers. Although new applications for AI in health care are being developed and are proceeding through Food and Drug Administration approvals at a rapid pace, hospitals and health systems face challenges in adopting them. Acquiring, learning and applying a new technology can require a large initial investment, and medical personnel may fear losing their jobs—just two factors that can delay its implementation.

The results of the latest *Futurescan* national survey show that health care executives are divided on the use of AI. While 44 percent of respondents think it very or somewhat likely that AI will play a role in at least half of the patient diagnoses made at their hospital or health system by 2025, 35 percent consider it unlikely.

Wearables and Quantified Health

Although Fitbit launched the wearables revolution just 10 years ago, health tracking devices are now mainstream. At first they simply documented fitness activities, but now that technology giants have entered the health care sector, the applications are expanding.

For instance, the Apple Watch now features both an atrial fibrillation–detecting algorithm and an electrocardiogram that helps identify heart abnormalities, and its Movement Disorder API is being used to monitor symptoms in patients with Parkinson's disease. Specialized wearables can track blood glucose levels and blood pressure, alerting the wearer of anomalies in the readings or texting medication reminders. The devices measure health metrics on an ongoing basis, detect numbers that may indicate an emerging health condition and transmit patient data to the wearers' clinicians.

In addition to wearables, virtual assistants such as Amazon's Alexa and modified Wi-Fi now provide the capability to continuously measure and report vital signs and other health markers. "I liken these technologies to a 'check engine'

committed to enhancing population health in their communities, Kraft says, the widespread use of wearables and other connected technologies that share health data is an important development in the successful transition to value-based reimbursement. Patient-centered medical homes across the country are leveraging connected devices to track the health status of patients with congestive heart failure, diabetes and hypertension, as well as those recovering from surgery. These strategies are helping to lower health care expenditures and improve outcomes.

Wearables can also play a role in predictive analytics, especially when combined with the power of AI in trending and forecasting health needs. The access to so much personal health information raises privacy concerns, however. Kraft says

Kraft says genomic medicine applications are helping to identify genetic factors that contribute to rare conditions and common illnesses such as diabetes, hypertension and cancer. Precision medicine is increasingly effective in treating certain types of cancer and can help predict how patients will respond to specific drugs and other therapies.

Nationwide Children's Hospital in Columbus, Ohio, was an early adopter of genomics-guided pediatric precision medicine. Since 2016, Nationwide Children's has expanded the availability of clinical genetic and genomic testing to diagnose pediatric conditions earlier, to better predict outcomes and to personalize treatment to individual patients. In these efforts, scientists and clinicians combine next generation sequencing–based assays with computational analysis pipelines to provide molecular diagnostic testing for medical genetics, cancer, epilepsy and other inherited conditions.

As the nation's health care system continues to evolve, so does the power of technology to better predict, prevent and cure disease and to change how, where and by whom care is delivered.

---

light in cars, but for the human body," says Kraft. "Together, they are creating a quantified health culture where people are becoming more aware, involved and responsible for their health."

Ochsner Health System in New Orleans has launched a digital health initiative for expectant women through its innovation lab, innovationOchsner. The Connected MOM (Maternity Online Monitoring) program provides remote pregnancy care via wireless blood pressure cuffs and scales and at-home urine tests that send real-time results to an obstetrician (OB). The ongoing virtual pregnancy surveillance has reduced OB office visits by 25–30 percent and has facilitated earlier diagnosis of preeclampsia in many pregnant women.

Considerations for providers. For health care organizations that have

that health systems must carefully evaluate and implement measures to safeguard patient data and protect it from unethical use and exploitation. Blockchain technologies are being explored to help circumvent privacy and security threats.

Genomic and Precision Medicine

Genomic medicine is an emerging medical discipline that uses DNA sequencing and genetic information about individuals to help make diagnostic and treatment decisions and to determine their predisposition to certain diseases. Precision medicine goes a step further, relying on a patient's genes, behaviors and environment to further personalize prevention, guide screening and diagnosis, and prescribe medical interventions.

Considerations for providers. As the cost of whole-genome sequencing has fallen dramatically in recent years, the technology is increasingly being used in community-based hospitals, not just academic medical centers. Its adoption does require health care organizations to build an information technology (IT) ecosystem that can leverage genomic medicine, Kraft acknowledges.

Other barriers to adoption include recruitment of specialized clinicians trained in this area and reengineering of clinical workflows. The biggest challenge, however, is reimbursement, notes Kraft. "Currently, genomics is not a seamless part of the clinical workflow, and establishing rates for diagnostic tests that reflect the value of the care has been difficult for payers."

Telehealth and Virtual Care

Currently, 76 percent of U.S. hospitals connect with patients and consulting practitioners through the use of video and other digital communication technologies (American Hospital Association 2019). Telehealth visits have grown substantially, from just 206 in 2005 to more than 202,000 in 2017, as a growing number of consumers—especially millennials—seek more convenient and cost-effective care options (Barnett, Ray and Souza 2018). Physician adoption of telehealth increased from 5 percent to 22 percent between 2015 and 2018, a survey of 800 physicians shows (American Well 2019).

Mount Sinai Health System in New York provides real-time stroke consults from its Queens facility for its outlying hospitals. Physicians specializing in stroke diagnosis and treatment use a state-of-the-art video telecommunications system to determine if immediate intervention is needed. Patients who meet certain criteria may receive immediate t-PA (tissue plasminogen activator) therapy to dissolve the blood clot and restore blood flow to the brain, or they may undergo endovascular therapies such as mechanical clot extraction.

Considerations for providers.
Telehealth services can be an important component in the delivery of value-based care because they expand patients' access to primary and specialty treatment. Although every state Medicaid program and many private insurers reimburse for telehealth services, Medicare generally still limits payment. Medicare payment for telehealth services also does not provide adequate compensation to all sites of care. "Telemedicine is more than just a clinician on a screen," notes Kraft. "It is moving to the use of home-based diagnostics, chatbots and synchronous monitoring to manage conditions on an ongoing basis."

For remote physician consultations, Kraft says, many rural hospitals need improved IT infrastructure and greater access to broadband technology. In addition, significant federal and state legal and regulatory issues related to licensing, credentialing, prescribing, professional liability insurance, privacy, and fraud and abuse need to be resolved.

Virtual Reality and Augmented Reality
"Many providers are already using these technologies in some capacity,"

explains Kraft. Virtual reality (VR) is being used to treat pain and provide education on conditions and treatment plans. It can help patients visualize how lifestyle modifications may yield tangible results in fitness, wellness and vitality. VR and augmented reality (AR) are helping train physicians in high-risk procedures via simulations of real-life scenarios. Kraft says AR is also being used to visualize tumors and deliver more precise cancer treatments.

New applications for AR and VR are rapidly being developed. The Stanford University School of Medicine is employing technology that uses headsets and combined images from magnetic resonance imaging, CT scans and angiograms to create 3-D interactive models that help clinicians and patients visualize and understand what will happen during surgeries. Stanford is also using its VR system to train residents through virtual procedures; facilitate presurgical planning; and guide surgeons in the operating room, improving accuracy.

Considerations for providers. As with other innovative health care technologies, implementing AR and VR poses challenges. Mainstreaming their use requires reengineering workflows and payment models (Holland 2019). In addition, clinicians may not understand how to use the technology

or when to use or prescribe it (BIS Research 2019).

Implications for Health Care Leaders
Whether and how hospitals and health systems incorporate innovations in medical technology and patient care will require careful consideration, evaluation and forward-thinking leadership. Kraft emphasizes that leaders will need to determine which advances are feasible for their organizations (from both a financial and physician/staff expertise perspective) and which offer the greatest benefit for the communities they serve. The considerations for providers included throughout this article can be an important starting point for discussion among C-suite executives, boards and medical staffs.

The latest *Futurescan* survey shows no consensus among U.S. health care executives on the degree to which they will embrace advances in medical technology and new approaches to health care. When asked if they agree that their hospital or health system will, by 2025, devote 50 percent or more of its efforts to wellness rather than treating disease, about half (48 percent) of respondents thought it somewhat or very unlikely, while 42 percent believed it somewhat or very likely.

As the Centers for Medicare & Medicaid Services and other payers continue to move the U.S. health care delivery system to models that prevent sickness and keep people healthy, leaders and frontline caregivers should identify the newest medical developments that will enable them to attain that goal. Kraft recommends that they take into account the following factors before moving forward with new technologies and care models in their organizations:

- Keep abreast of cutting-edge advances in medicine, especially in specialties offered by a hospital or health system. "This may be an appropriate assignment for the chief technology or innovation officer, or a reason to add such a position if an organization doesn't have one," Kraft advises.

- Monitor reimbursement scenarios for new innovations as they evolve at the state and federal levels. Payment models can vary depending on the payers in a particular region.
- Project if medical breakthroughs will have service line implications for the health care organization. Some innovations, such as new cancer treatments, may obviate the need for additional investments in inpatient facilities, infusion centers or other specialty-driven infrastructure.

Conclusion

As the nation's health care system continues to evolve, so does the power of technology to better predict, prevent and cure disease and to change how, where and by whom care is delivered. What the disparate innovations highlighted in this article have in common is the use of digital connectivity to improve lives. "I appreciate these medical advances for what they are: new means to create increasingly useful, real-time personalized connectedness in health care," says Kraft. "Our challenge going forward will be to maximize the potential of these tools and continue improving the science of medicine for the benefit of patients everywhere."

References

American Hospital Association. 2019. "Fact Sheet: Telehealth." Published February. www.aha.org/system/files/2019-02/fact-sheet-telehealth-2-4-19.pdf.

American Well. 2019. "Telehealth Index: 2019 Physician Survey." Accessed November 11. https://static.americanwell.com/app/uploads/2019/04/American-Well-Telehealth-Index-2019-Physician-Survey.pdf.

Barnett, M.L., K.N. Ray and J. Souza. 2018. "Trends in Telemedicine Use in a Large Commercially Insured Population, 2005–2017." *Journal of the American Medical Association* 320 (20): 2147–49.

BIS Research. 2019. "Virtual Reality and Augmented Reality in Healthcare: A Market Overview." Published May 22. https://blog.marketresearch.com/virtual-reality-and-augmented-reality-in-healthcare-a-market-overview.

Holland, M. 2019. "VR in Healthcare Is Changing the Patient Care Game." TechTarget. Published January 21. https://searchhealthit.techtarget.com/feature/VR-in-healthcare-is-changing-the-patient-care-game.

Frictionless Health Care Requires a Connected Healing Ecosystem

with M. Bridget Duffy, M.D.

In an age of unprecedented consumerism, hospitals and health systems looking for long-term sustainability need to make a frictionless patient experience the new strategic imperative.

What exactly comprises a frictionless health care journey? "Quite simply, it is creating a consistent, seamless experience of care from first impression to last where every person is treated with compassion and competence," says M. Bridget Duffy, M.D., chief medical officer of Vocera Communications Inc., one of the nation's foremost authorities and thought leaders on the patient and care team experience. "It requires a connected healing ecosystem of people, processes and technology that fosters respect and empathy, builds trusted relationships, eases suffering and restores humanity to health care."

The Challenging New Health Care Landscape

Duffy says several trends are converging to make designing a frictionless health care experience vital to the future success of health care organizations:

- The digital health revolution with "Amazon-level" service has

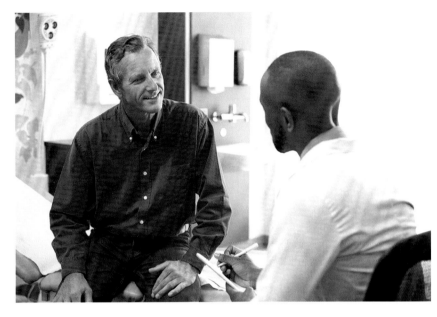

heightened patient expectations for personalization and convenience. Patient experience is five times more likely to influence system loyalty than traditional brand promotion is (Press Ganey 2018).

- The consumerization of health care is changing the way people make health care purchasing decisions, especially as high-deductible health plans force many Americans to pay out of pocket for once-covered services. The average

family's health care expenditures increased 18 percent from 2013 to 2018, far surpassing the 8 percent increase in inflation and the 12 percent increase in workers' wages over the same period (Rae, Copeland and Cox 2019).

- The expansion of care outside hospitals and clinics will require new technologies and transmission of critical data. Building virtual relationships and trust will be the key to patient loyalty.

About the Subject Matter Expert

M. Bridget Duffy, M.D., is the chief medical officer of Vocera Communications Inc., where she plays a key role in new product innovation and accelerating the adoption of technology that restores the patient's voice to health care, improves physician and nurse communication, and eases the burden of being a clinician. She also is a co-founder of the company's Experience Innovation Network, an international group of clinicians, patient advocates, innovators, hospital executives and other industry leaders focused on finding innovative ways to

humanize health care. Duffy's journey from medical school at the University of Minnesota to an internal medicine residency at Abbott Northwestern Hospital inspired a diverse career path. She was an early pioneer in the creation of hospitalist medicine and was the nation's first health care chief experience officer, establishing that role at the Cleveland Clinic. For more than 25 years, she has been disrupting the status quo and leading a movement to restore human connections and improve the health care experience for all.

FUTURESCAN SURVEY RESULTS
Frictionless Health Care

Health care executives from across the nation were asked how likely it is that the following will happen in their hospital or health system within the next five years.

By 2025, our hospital or health system will increase the time that physicians spend with patients by adopting systems that reduce the amount of time spent on nonclinical procedures and processes.

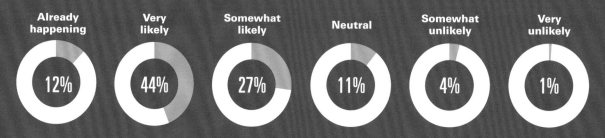

Already happening	Very likely	Somewhat likely	Neutral	Somewhat unlikely	Very unlikely
12%	44%	27%	11%	4%	1%

By 2025, our hospital or health system will improve patient health outcomes by adopting systems that reduce the amount of time spent on nonclinical procedures and processes.

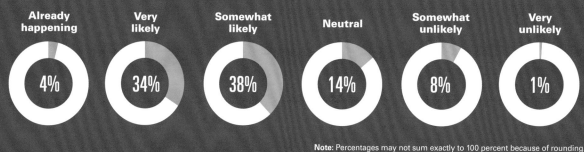

Already happening	Very likely	Somewhat likely	Neutral	Somewhat unlikely	Very unlikely
4%	34%	38%	14%	8%	1%

Note: Percentages may not sum exactly to 100 percent because of rounding.

- The epidemic of cognitive overload and burnout among clinicians has become a public health crisis that is directly affecting the quality of care and patient safety across the care continuum. More than 40 percent of physicians are burned out, with doctors in some specialties suffering more than those in others (Medscape 2019). Clinician distraction has been shown to play a role in nearly 75 percent of medical errors (Tariq and Scherbak 2019), which cause more than 250,000 deaths each year in the United States (Makary and Daniel 2016). Cognitive overload is also a cause in 80 percent of medical device user errors (Faiola, Srinivas and Duke 2015).

"Clearly, the onus is on leaders to create a seamless experience, from the first point of contact with patients through aftercare, that enables better human connections and drives improved outcomes," explains Duffy. "Doing this also requires removing friction for our care teams and creating environments that protect the emotional and physical well-being of physicians, nurses and frontline staff."

Implications for Health Care Leaders

Health care leaders can approach these challenges from a number of perspectives. The following strategies have proven effective in diverse organizations across the country.

Build a human-centered leadership and culture. "To eliminate friction from health care, hospital and health system CEOs and other members of the C-suite must create a culture that values a human-centered approach to innovation," says Duffy. "There must be a top-down and bottom-up commitment to identify opportunities to improve the experience from the provider, patient and family perspectives. We must remove preventable sources of frustration from the system, and that starts by building a culture that is committed to removing administrative and bureaucratic hassles."

A human-centered culture emphasizes the following:

- A connected care team that communicates effectively with patients and each other.
- Collegiality and respect among the diverse disciplines and professions represented.
- Efficient clinical and operational processes and workflows.
- Implementation of technology that fosters a sacred, healing relationship between providers and patients.

Involve diverse patient and family voices. In creating a frictionless experience, health care leaders should place a greater focus on patients' and family members' personal preferences at every stage of care. "They need to identify and address pain points, as well as understand the moments that most touched their hearts so that those experiences can be scaled," stresses Duffy. "Doing so involves addressing health literacy and disparities and having cultural humility."

One research study found variances in how organizations integrate patient and family perspectives, influence and advocacy into strategies to enhance health care (Experience Innovation Network 2018). Although most organizations obtain their feedback via surveys and advisory councils, a few have gone further by partnering with patients and families as "true co-architects of innovation and transformation," says Duffy, noting that the most effective approaches involve integrating them into project teams, leadership forums and process improvement initiatives. Some progressive providers have even involved

patients extensively in experience design and design sprints.

Key tools for measuring the results of frictionless care initiatives include patient safety and satisfaction metrics that are linked to reimbursement. "Consistently low scores on patient experience have a direct and negative impact on the bottom line," notes Duffy. In contrast, health care organizations that emphasize compassion benefit from better financial performance and higher patient and caregiver satisfaction (Schwartz Center for Compassionate Healthcare 2015).

Insights that can be gleaned from patient and family posts on social media should also be analyzed on a regular basis to identify opportunities for improvement.

Deploy technology and systems that optimize the clinician experience. Health care organizations must also concentrate on removing friction from clinical workflows. "Minimizing hassles and interruptions for nurses and doctors—such as time-consuming documentation in electronic medical records (EMRs)—will give them back valuable time to do what they are passionate about and what brings them joy: caring for people," notes Duffy, who says the additional burden created by EMRs is contributing to

clinician cognitive overload. To address the problem, she says, leaders should consider quantifying the impact of new technology on caregivers and focus on implementing digital tools that streamline processes, such as voice-enabled documentation.

The results of the latest *Futurescan* survey indicate that health care executives across the country are getting the message. Nearly three-quarters (71 percent) of respondents indicate it is somewhat to very likely that by 2025, their hospital or health system will have increased the time doctors spend with patients by adopting systems that reduce the amount of time spent on nonclinical procedures and processes. Another 12 percent say they have already done so. Additionally, 72 percent of survey respondents believe that taking such steps will lead to improved patient outcomes.

When a new technology or process is implemented, Duffy says, it is important to measure staff well-being and clinician resilience before and after the solution is deployed. "Pre- and post-measurements let hospitals know if they are designing an ideal working environment for care teams and an ideal healing environment for patients," says Duffy. "Metrics also enable health care leaders to make changes as needed before fatigue and frustration set in and affect a health system's operations and culture."

Human-Centered Best Practices for a Frictionless Connected Healing Ecosystem

In today's environment, more providers are embracing the principles of patient- and family-centered care and finding it to be good medicine. A scientific literature review undertaken by Dignity Health (2014) and the Center for Compassion and Altruism Research and Education at the Stanford University School of Medicine found that when health care workers treat patients with compassion, the patients often heal faster and have less pain and anxiety. Duffy cites the following best practices from organizations she says are already working toward restoring humanity to health care.

33rd percentile for patient satisfaction on the HCAHPS (Hospital Consumer Assessment of Healthcare Providers and Systems) survey. Leadership engaged in a robust mapping process to determine key dissatisfiers in the patient experience. One outcome was the development of a sacred-moments program, which contributed to a 117 percent increase in overall patient satisfaction scores.

Code Lavender™. Like a code blue that is called when a patient needs emergency medical attention, a Code Lavender signals the need for deploying a rapid-response team to address the emotional, spiritual or physical needs of patients, family members or hospital staff. "As cognitive overload, burnout and fatigue reach a tipping point for caregivers, Code Lavender helps to remind them that the organi-

to bring a more humanistic approach to informed consent. "Informed hope" not only enables patients to understand the risks of interventional procedures and surgeries but also gives them a chance to ask questions and express their fears, concerns and hopes. "This process takes little time or effort, yet it provides the peace of mind that can have a significant impact on a patient's experience, healing and outcomes," observes Duffy.

Marc R. Katz, M.D., a cardiac surgeon in Charleston, South Carolina, standardized the use of informed hope in his medical practice prior to performing heart surgery. "Informed hope helps patients make educated decisions about their care and proceed with confidence and a positive spirit, both of which are fundamental to achieving good outcomes," says Katz.

Health care organizations that emphasize compassion benefit from better financial performance and higher patient and caregiver satisfaction.

Sacred moments. When a patient is admitted to the hospital, the conversation tends to focus on the physical ailment, insurance issues, living wills and the like. These interactions are important, but they overlook the fact that every patient is a human being with concerns and needs that extend beyond the procedure and payment. Implementing a "sacred moment" at admission offers time for a doctor, nurse or other member of the care team to ask patients critical questions about their fears, spiritual desires and communication preferences; inspires a greater connection with patients; and improves the patient experience. It also helps restore a sense of purpose for staff.

Several years ago, a medical center in Missouri found itself ranked in the

zation cares about their well-being," says Duffy.

At a children's hospital in California, Code Lavender supports those involved in an adverse event or when a medical error occurs. When an alert is called, therapists, chaplains and other personnel respond to give emotional support to the entire team and family involved in the incident. Six months after launching the program, the team reported substantial improvement in employee engagement and loyalty, as well as a sharp decline (from 24 percent to 3 percent) in the proportion of staff members reporting that they "do not feel supported" by the organization.

Informed hope. This clinical standard advocated by Duffy is designed

Conclusion

To prepare for the future in the new era of consumerism, Duffy says, hospital and health system leaders need to place greater emphasis on developing a frictionless experience for patients, families and clinical teams. "This will require increased efforts to proactively obtain their feedback and input and involve them in a human-centered design process," notes Duffy. "It will also require establishing new, hardwired clinical standards that humanize the patient experience from before arrival to after discharge."

Duffy also points to the need to engage staff and patients in technology decisions and to find metrics to assess how well new process improvements and technology facilitate human connections in medicine that extend beyond hospital and clinic settings and support patients on their journey. "Health care leaders who partner with patients to establish a truly healing ecosystem will not only earn patient loyalty but also empower their clinicians to return to their true purpose: enabling people to heal."

References

Dignity Health. 2014. "Scientific Literature Review Shows Health Care Delivered with Kindness and Compassion Leads to Faster Healing, Reduced Pain." Published November 12. www.dignityhealth.org/about-us/press-center/press-releases/scientific-literature-review-with-stanford.

Experience Innovation Network. 2018. "Co-Architecting Healthcare Transformation: How Leading Health Systems Put Patients and Families at the Forefront of Design." Accessed November 1, 2019. www.vocera.com/sites/default/files/CoArchitectinHealthcareTransformation.pdf.

Faiola, A., P. Srinivas and J. Duke. 2015. "Supporting Clinical Cognition: A Human-Centered Approach to a Novel ICU Information Visualization Dashboard." *American Medical Information Association Annual Symposium Proceedings*. Published November 5. www.ncbi.nlm.nih.gov/pmc/articles/PMC4765655/.

Makary, M.A., and M. Daniel. 2016. "Medical Error—the Third Leading Cause of Death in the U.S." *British Medical Journal* 353: i2139.

Medscape. 2019. *National Physician Burnout, Depression and Suicide Report*. Published January 16. www.medscape.com/slideshow/2019-lifestyle-burnout-depression-6011056.

Press Ganey. 2018. *Consumerism: The Role of Patient Experience in Brand Management and Patient Acquisition*. South Bend, IN: Press Ganey Associates Inc.

Rae, M., R. Copeland and C. Cox. 2019. "Tracking the Rise in Premium Contributions and Cost-Sharing for Families with Large Employer Coverage." Peterson-Kaiser Health System Tracker. Published August 14. www.healthsystemtracker.org/?sfid=4356.

Schwartz Center for Compassionate Healthcare. 2015. "Building Compassion into the Bottom Line: The Role of Compassionate Care and Patient Experience in 35 U.S. Hospitals and Health Systems." Published March. www.theschwartzcenter.org/wp-content/uploads/2019/06/Building-Compassion-into-the-Bottom-Line.pdf.

Tariq, R.A., and Y. Scherbak. 2019. "Medication Errors." National Center for Biotechnology Information. Published January. www.ncbi.nlm.nih.gov/books/NBK519065/.

A Five-Part Solution to Healthy Aging in America

with Ken Dychtwald, Ph.D.

Two parallel trends are dramatically affecting the future of health care delivery for older adults in the United States: (1) the aging of the baby boomer generation and (2) the growing number of elderly men and women who require intensive medical services. Identifying strategies to effectively address these trends—and the implications they hold for society overall—will be a major challenge for hospitals and health systems over the next five years and beyond.

"Because of breakthroughs in medicine and health care, many previously fatal diseases can now be controlled or have been eradicated," says Ken Dychtwald, Ph.D., one of the foremost thought leaders on issues relating to the aging population and the founder of Age Wave. "We have large numbers of people living into their 80s and 90s, and a disproportionate share of health and medical expenditures are devoted to caring for the elderly. Yet, with all the money our nation spends on health care, there are 33 other countries whose mortality and longevity rates are better than those of the United States," Dychtwald explains (World Health Organization 2018). "In light of these statistics, an important question that

needs to be asked is: What do we need to do to match Americans' health span with their life span?"

Key Challenges Facing the Health Care Field

In projecting how care will be delivered in the future to maximize the health and wellness of the aged, Dychtwald highlights the following key concepts that hospital and health system executives should be aware of and prepared for.

Demography is destiny—the age wave is coming. Tens of millions of baby boomers are retired or are nearing retirement. "This new generation of older adults is going to live longer and age differently than their parents and grandparents did," says Dychtwald. "Their expectations are going to require providers to adapt to meet their demands." Boomers will be more:

- Proactive about their health, with a keen interest in wellness.

About the Subject Matter Expert

Over the course of more than 40 years, Ken Dychtwald, Ph.D., has emerged as North America's foremost visionary and thought leader regarding the health care, economic, marketing and workforce implications of the "age wave." Dychtwald is a psychologist, gerontologist and best-selling author of 16 books, including *Age Wave, The Role of the Hospital in an Aging Society, Healthy Aging*, and *A New Purpose*. Since 1986, Dychtwald has been the founding CEO of Age Wave, whose client list has included more than half of the *Fortune* 500 list of companies. He has served as a fellow of the World Economic Forum and was a featured speaker at two White House Conferences on Aging. Dychtwald has twice received the American Society on Aging Award for outstanding national leadership. He also serves as chairman of the Alzheimer's XPRIZE initiative.

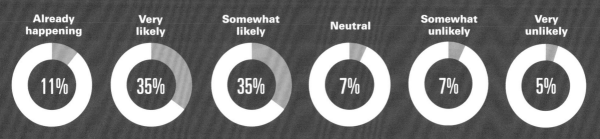
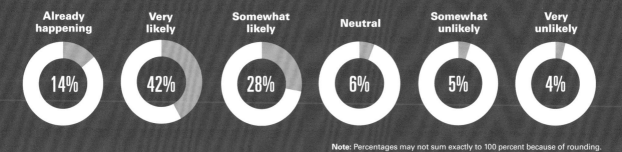
- Interested in prolonging "healthy living."
- Selective about where they live, including a preference for aging at home or in cohousing communities rather than in assisted living facilities or nursing homes.
- Involved in decision-making about their medical care.
- Discerning in their choice of physicians and hospitals, with high expectations for the patient experience.

Our concept of "old" is getting older. According to data from the Centers for Disease Control and Prevention's National Center for Health Statistics, the 15 percent of our population aged 65 or older already accounts for 31 percent of all doctor's office visits, 38 percent of all hospital stays and 45 percent of inpatient days of care (Levant, Chari and DeFrances 2015; National Center for Health Statistics 2017). However, the "oldest of the old," defined as the demographic aged 85 and older, is growing faster than any other age group. In 1900, only 122,362 people were aged 85 or older in the United States. Today, 6.4 million Americans are 85 or older (Administration for Community Living and Administration on Aging 2018). This age cohort is consuming an ever-increasing share of medical resources, particularly when it comes to treating comorbidities and providing end-of-life care.

Life span does not equal health span. "Although better medical care has managed to prolong the life span of many Americans, it has not necessarily prolonged their health span," Dychtwald notes. The nation has legions of baby boomers and long-lived elders who struggle with chronic, degenerative health problems such as heart disease, cancer, Alzheimer's disease, stroke and diabetes. A disproportionate share of health care resources is spent on medical care for the aging population.

Implications for Health Care Leaders: A Five-Part Solution

"To meet the needs of aging baby boomers and avert the chronic disease epidemic looming in the future for the oldest old, we must establish an overarching, long-term commitment to replace unhealthy aging with healthy aging," says Dychtwald. This includes placing a greater emphasis on maximizing health, finding scientific breakthroughs, improving wellness, preventing diseases and enacting early interventions to more effectively manage chronic conditions. Dychtwald suggests that an investment in human, intellectual and capital resources will be required to achieve

worn and used by older Americans, many of whom find traditional personal emergency response systems stigmatizing," he says.

As another example, Pillo is a medication management robot that gives medication reminders, tracks if and when pills are taken and orders refills. Xandar Kardian offers a contact-free, radar-enabled device that keeps track of a user's vital signs and can detect a fall. And Care Predict created a machine-learning wearable that uses kinematics to quantify daily activities, predict health conditions and monitor vital signs.

Health care executives can facilitate the delivery of these technologies and

dementia have twice as many hospital stays per year as other older people and are more likely to have chronic conditions such as heart disease, diabetes and kidney disease.

Last year, Alzheimer's and other types of dementia cost the nation $290 billion, including $195 billion in Medicare and Medicaid payments. Unless a treatment to slow, stop or prevent the disease is developed, Alzheimer's is projected to cost more than $1.1 trillion (in 2019 dollars) by 2050. This dramatic rise includes more-than-fourfold increases in both government spending under Medicare and Medicaid and out-of-pocket spending (Alzheimer's Association 2019). It is estimated that postponing the onset of Alzheimer's by five years would decrease the incidence of the disease by 50 percent and sharply reduce the need for nursing home care in the United States (Butler 2008). "Without advances in the battle against Alzheimer's, the breakthroughs that postpone or eliminate heart disease, cancer, stroke, diabetes and other illnesses will inadvertently create more longer-lived but cognitively impaired aging adults," Dychtwald stresses. To address the issue, he says, the nation's health care system must promote the scientific research needed to cure or delay the effects of Alzheimer's. Hospitals and health systems can participate in this quest by:

> As the nation's population grows older, providers at all levels will need to initiate innovative approaches to caring for older adults and promoting their health and wellness.

these goals by focusing on the following five-part solution.

1. Use advances in medicine and technology to develop innovative solutions for healthy aging. As companies such as Amazon, Apple and Google continue to enter the health care sector, Dychtwald says they will dramatically change where and how health care is delivered through advances in technology, such as home monitoring systems, health and medical apps, voice assistants, telemedicine, personal emergency response systems, artificial intelligence and virtual medicine.

"For elderly individuals with mobility or transportation difficulties, these technologies can be game changers in helping them maintain their health and independence," observes Dychtwald. The Apple Watch now comes with fall detection and the ability to monitor heart irregularities. "Because these watches do so much beyond health monitoring, they're more likely to be

encourage physicians, health plans and caregivers to use them with older adults. This strategy aligns with the central role that health systems see for themselves in coordinating their community's long-term health care for an aging population. According to the *Futurescan* national survey, 81 percent of responding hospital and health system leaders say they already are taking on this mission or are somewhat to very likely to do so by 2025.

2. Promote research to reverse or cure Alzheimer's disease. Alzheimer's disease is the sixth leading cause of death in the United States, and the only one on the rise because there is no cure (Alzheimer's Association 2019). Yet only 16 percent of seniors receive regular cognitive assessments during their routine check-ups, versus 91 percent who receive hypertension screenings and 83 percent who have cholesterol checks (Alzheimer's Association 2019). People living with Alzheimer's or other types of

- Providing evidence-based, best-practice Alzheimer's services and treatments to help optimize life for those with the disease.
- Participating in or supporting Alzheimer's research.
- Establishing community-based Alzheimer's programs and clinics that raise awareness, destigmatize dementia, promote early diagnosis and provide effective treatments to prolong quality of life.

3. Find and recruit health care professionals specializing in gerontology. Although leaders in this field disagree as to how many geriatric specialists will be needed in the future, there is strong consensus that health care professionals will need an array of basic skills to provide the complex care that older patients require. The projected shortage of physicians, nurses and other health care professionals will exacerbate the problem of access to care for this population. Hospitals and health systems can address these issues by:

- Taking action to alleviate the workforce shortage through innovative recruitment, hiring and retention strategies.
- Helping doctors and nurses acquire the skills to provide specialized care to the elderly through geriatric and longevity-related continuing education.
- Developing programs and facilities to meet the needs of older Americans, such as Alzheimer's treatment centers.

"One way to build geriatric competencies is through programs like the American College of Emergency Physicians' Geriatric Emergency Department Accreditation program," says Dychtwald. For accreditation, staff must meet certain geriatric training criteria, in addition to procedural and structural requirements. As of November 2019, 107 hospitals had achieved accreditation and another 225 hospitals had applied for accreditation.

Another promising approach is educational partnerships with health associations that focus on diseases affecting the aged. For instance, the Colorado Department of Public Health and Environment partnered with the Alzheimer's Association to develop a one-day, in-person course for emergency medical providers on how to effectively assist people with Alzheimer's and other types of dementia—something many first responders previously had little to no formal training in.

4. Make lifelong disease prevention, management of chronic diseases and self-care national priorities. "As we have transitioned our focus from acute

infectious diseases to chronic diseases, we've learned that a sizable contributor to people's potential for lifelong health are their own personal behaviors, not historically the domain of hospitals," observes Dychtwald. However, many of the oldest old grew up unaware of the detrimental effects of smoking, a high-fat diet and a sedentary lifestyle. "Many have simply taken very poor care of themselves," Dychtwald explains. Fortunately, the movement toward population health has inspired hospitals and health systems to take leadership roles in creating healthier communities. The results of the *Futurescan* survey indicate that 14 percent of responding executives say their hospital or health system is already leading formal, community-wide initiatives to promote healthy aging, and another 70 percent plan to do so by 2025. But there is more to be done, and hospitals and health systems can make an impact by:

- Creating education and wellness programs specifically for aging adults.
- Implementing best practices in helping the elderly address personal behaviors that put their health at risk.
- Implementing better multidisciplinary care and care coordination for older patients.

5. Develop a humane approach to the end of life. "When the end of life is near, the aged should be allowed to retain as much control as possible over their death," stresses Dychtwald. "This includes having access to spiritual and emotional support, enacting advance directives to ensure their final wishes are respected, taking steps to minimize discomfort or suffering and dying with dignity." Hospitals and health systems can help ensure a humane approach to the end of life through the provision of:

- Palliative and hospice care programs.
- Education for older adults and their families on advance directives.
- Education for caregivers on the end-of-life options available to their loved ones.

Conclusion

As the nation's population grows older, providers at all levels will need to initiate innovative approaches to caring for older adults and promoting their health and wellness. Hospitals and health systems will also have to adapt to the changing needs and expectations of aging baby boomers. By embracing the five-part solution outlined in this article, health care executives can help align the health span of elderly Americans with their life span—and create a new blueprint for healthy aging in the United States.

References

Administration for Community Living and Administration on Aging. 2018. *2017 Profile of Older Americans*. Published April. https://acl.gov/sites/default/files/Aging%20and%20Disability%20in%20America/2017OlderAmericansProfile.pdf.

Alzheimer's Association. 2019. *2019 Alzheimer's Disease Facts and Figures*. Accessed October 3. www.alz.org/media/documents/alzheimers-facts-and-figures-2019-r.pdf.

Butler, R.N. 2008. *The Longevity Revolution: The Benefits and Challenges of Living a Long Life*. New York: PublicAffairs.

Levant, S., K. Chari, and C.J. DeFrances. 2015. "Hospitalizations for Patients Aged 85 and Over in the United States, 2000–2010." National Center for Health Statistics. Published January. www.cdc.gov/nchs/data/databriefs/db182.pdf.

National Center for Health Statistics. 2017. "Visits to Physician Offices, Hospital Outpatient Departments, and Hospital Emergency Departments, by Age, Sex, and Race: United States, Selected Years 2000–2015." Accessed October 3, 2019. www.ncbi.nlm.nih.gov/books/NBK532684/bin/t1-ch4.t76.pdf.

World Health Organization. 2018. "Life Expectancy and Healthy Life Expectancy: Data by Country." Updated April 6. http://apps.who.int/gho/data/view.main.SDG2016LEXv.

Innovation Is Key to the Future Viability of Medicaid

with Andy Slavitt

Medicaid, the largest health insurer in the United States, is facing increasingly complicated challenges that threaten the future of the program at a time when the needs of key stakeholders are growing on multiple fronts.

From beneficiaries' greater reliance on Medicaid for basic and acute medical needs, to providers' difficulty in sustaining operating margins based on reimbursement rates, to federal and state governments' inability to afford the program's scale, obstacles abound. Overcoming them and securing the long-term viability of the program will require Medicaid and hospital and health system leaders to evolve and bring innovative solutions to the forefront.

A Program Under Attack

The statistics associated with Medicaid are staggering: The program covers one in five Americans and nearly half of all births. It is the primary source of long-term care coverage and now accounts for nearly 20 percent of all personal health spending in the United States. And it does all this at a lower per capita cost than any other health care program in the country, while achieving high patient satisfaction scores (Rudowitz, Garfield and Hinton 2019). Yet according to Andy Slavitt, former acting administrator for the Centers for Medicare & Medicaid Services, Medicaid is continually under political attack "despite the fact that it is, by any measure, a widely successful program."

The greatest change to Medicaid since its founding more than 50 years ago came with the Affordable Care Act (ACA), which called for states to expand Medicaid access to all adults under age 65 with incomes below 138 percent of the federal poverty level. To date, 37 states including the District of Columbia have expanded Medicaid coverage (exhibit 1).

About the Subject Matter Expert

Andy Slavitt served as acting administrator for the Centers for Medicare & Medicaid Services under President Obama from 2015 to 2017, overseeing Medicaid and Medicare, the Children's Health Insurance Program, value-based payment reform and the health insurance marketplace. Previously, he oversaw the successful turnaround of HealthCare.gov and served as a group executive vice president of Optum, which he led from inception to $35 billion in revenues. Slavitt is currently board chair of United States of Care, a national nonprofit health think tank and advocacy organization he founded to provide health care for all Americans. He co-chairs the Future of Healthcare initiative at the Bipartisan Policy Center and chairs the Medicaid Transformation Project, which aims to transform care for the most vulnerable populations. Slavitt is also the founder and general partner of Town Hall Ventures, which invests in health care innovations in vulnerable communities. He was named to *Politico Magazine*'s Politico 50 list; was recognized by *Modern Healthcare* as one of the 10 Most Influential People in Health Care; and was named the Most Influential Healthcare Tweeter by Healthcare Dive. Slavitt received bachelor of arts and bachelor of science degrees from the University of Pennsylvania and a master of business administration degree from Harvard University.

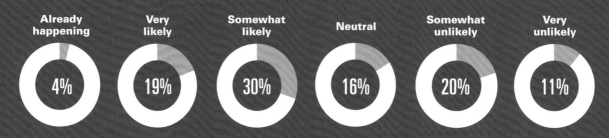
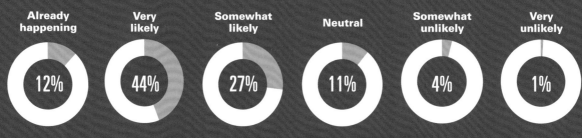
States that expanded Medicaid benefited from increased coverage, service use and quality of care, with little evidence of any negative consequences. For instance, wait times for providers did not increase (Mazurenko et al. 2018). At the same time, Medicaid spending is trending about 30 percent lower than expected since the program's expansion under the ACA, with overall spending per enrollee growing more slowly than private spending (Glied and Tavenner 2019).

Hospitals in expansion states have also reaped rewards such as the following (Antonisse et al. 2019):

- Fewer uninsured visits and lower uncompensated care costs.
- Improved patterns in emergency department use.
- Significantly reduced variation in the provision of uncompensated care among hospitals that treat a disproportionate share of low-income patients.
- Improved financial performance, including operating margins.

That is not to say Medicaid can't be improved, says Slavitt. "There is a lot of opportunity to continue to reform the program."

Addressing Funding and Access Concerns

Despite slower-than-expected spending growth, the greatest challenge that states face remains Medicaid funding, particularly as the federal government's contributions to the expansion decrease through 2020. "This is a big line item in their budgets, and there isn't enormous flexibility," emphasizes Slavitt. One way states raise money to pay for Medicaid is by imposing taxes on providers, and the majority of states that expanded Medicaid plan to increase taxes as the federal share drops (Kaiser Family Foundation 2017).

Exhibit 1

Status of State Action on Medicaid Expansion as of 2019

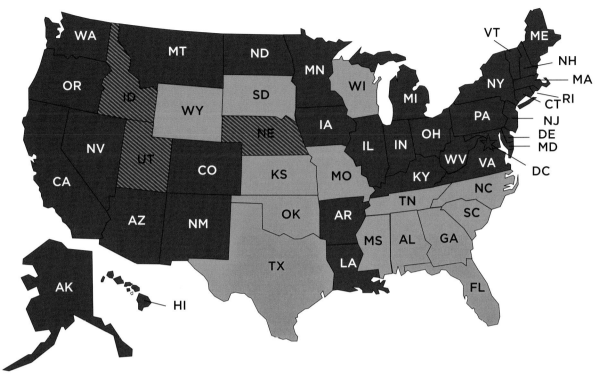

Adopted and implemented **Adopted but not implemented** **Not adopted**

Source: Kaiser Family Foundation (2019).

Slavitt maintains that Medicaid is chronically underfunded, which often results in reduced benefits for recipients or lower reimbursements for providers. This, in turn, can affect access to specialty care. "If a child has severe asthma and can't see an allergist for 90 days," Slavitt says, "then the program is failing that child and family as well as the state." Indeed, in a survey of nearly a hundred Medicaid managed care plans representing 31 of 39 states that use such plans, 80 percent of respondents indicated they had trouble recruiting specialists, compared to just 40 percent reporting difficulties in recruiting primary care physicians. Many are increasing payment rates to address the problem, and nearly 70 percent are now using telemedicine in at least one clinical area (Garfield et al. 2018).

However, access is also about culturally competent physicians and health systems that view it as part of their mission to take care of the most vulnerable populations. "I wish I could say all providers have the same level of commitment, but some simply do not want to accept Medicaid patients," Slavitt says. "Conversely, I've seen many that, despite the challenges, wouldn't dream of not seeing Medicaid patients because they consider it part of their obligation as clinicians."

Implications for Health Care Leaders

What role can hospitals and health systems play in addressing the challenges facing the Medicaid program and its beneficiaries now and in the future? Slavitt says there are two key areas providers should concentrate on.

Social determinants of health. One way to help manage costs is to think in terms of what the Medicaid population needs to be healthy. That means addressing social determinants of health, Slavitt says, including education, housing, transportation and food security.

Studies have found that environmental and socioeconomic factors are responsible for 50 percent of health, while access to quality health care accounts for just 20 percent. The remaining 30 percent is determined by behaviors such as smoking, physical activity and alcohol use (County Health Rankings and Roadmaps 2019).

Slavitt believes these factors are particularly important in the Medicaid population. About a third of Medicaid beneficiaries have less than a high school education, increasing their risk for disease and disability, and their low incomes make them more likely to encounter food and housing insecurity, high-stress environments

makes personalized recommendations of community resources based on patient location and language spoken, among other considerations (Dietsche 2019).

These approaches can produce significant savings. Montefiore's Housing at Risk program has realized annual returns-on-investment of 300 percent or more since it began (Morse 2018). In addition, a recent study of 1,073 Medicaid managed care patients found that the average medical costs of those whose social needs were met (e.g., medical transportation, utility payments, food pantries) fell an average of 22 percent ($6,653) in the first year (Pruitt et al. 2018).

"Most health care leaders think about the commercial population as being profitable and believe they lose money on Medicaid," Slavitt says. "They need to change their mind-set about how they serve the Medicaid population and focus on implementing solutions outside the walls of the hospital."

Medicaid transformation. Slavitt is leading a national movement to transform Medicaid from outside the federal and state systems. In 2018, he and AVIA Health Innovation created

(e.g., interpersonal violence) and difficulty accessing transportation to visit medical providers. They are also more apt to engage in unhealthy behaviors such as smoking or alcohol and substance abuse (Daniel-Robinson and Moore 2019).

Several health systems around the country have taken the lead in addressing social determinants of health. Bronx-based Montefiore Medical System, for instance, connects discharged patients who are homeless or at risk of becoming homeless with social workers who help them find safe housing (Morse 2018).

Another example is Northwell Health, based in New Hyde Park, New York, which recently partnered with Chicago-based NowPow to address the nonmedical needs of 1,200 high-risk Medicaid patients. NowPow offers a digital platform that mines diagnostic codes to identify patient needs, such as a lack of access to healthy food for those with diabetes, and then

What About Work Requirements?

The past couple of years have seen much debate and state action related to so-called "1115 waivers," which allow states to impose work requirements as a condition of eligibility for Medicaid recipients.

Critics point to the hardship that work requirements create for Medicaid beneficiaries, who often work hourly jobs with irregular schedules. As Slavitt (2018) wrote in an editorial for the *Journal of the American Medical Association*, "In practice, rather than increase the workforce by incentivizing . . . individuals, work requirements would harm three groups of people: the many who work, but can't maintain consistent hours to meet standards; those with disabilities that aren't recognized by the state; and many individuals who would be caught in a web of administrative paperwork under new systems being designed to monitor people's work and other habits." One analysis estimated that nearly half of all working adults currently covered under Medicaid would lose coverage in states that implemented work requirements (Aron-Dine, Chaudhry and Broaddus 2018).

Instead of work requirements, Slavitt recommends programs such as Montana's, which in 2016 linked Medicaid expansion and coverage to voluntary job training, placement and advancement rather than mandatory work requirements.

the Medicaid Transformation Project, funded in part by his venture capital firm Town Hall Ventures.

By November 2019, 29 health systems representing more than 350 hospitals in 25 states had joined the project, which seeks to leverage innovative digital solutions to encourage and support health systems as they take on Medicaid challenges such as the following:

- Integrating behavioral health screenings into primary care sites and improving access to mental health care for the approximately 9 million adult Medicaid beneficiaries with mental illness.
- Improving the infrastructure and organization of substance abuse treatment and recovery.
- Improving maternal care to improve infant health.
- Improving access to appropriate and timely emergency care in lower-cost and lower-acuity care settings to reduce emergency department visits.

Town Hall Ventures is also investing in companies designed to improve the health of underserved populations, particularly Medicaid beneficiaries. These companies include:

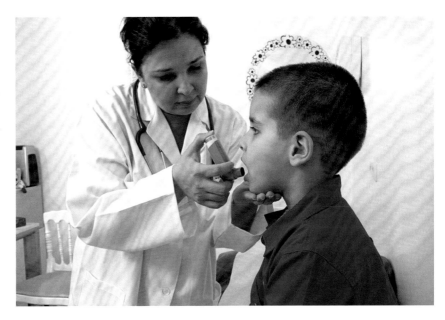

- Landmark, which provides home-based care to high-acuity Medicare and Medicaid beneficiaries, as well as dual-eligible individuals.
- CityBlock, a company that provides primary care and behavioral health and human services to address unmet needs in urban populations.
- Somatus and Strive Health, both of which focus on chronic kidney disease.

Slavitt also highlights the importance of health care equity. Rather than measuring how well providers are doing at meeting the objectives of the Institute for Healthcare Improvement's Triple Aim across a population, Slavitt says, "they should measure the gap between the best and worst care and concentrate on improving patient outcomes for those in the latter category. This will help leaders think differently about how resources are allocated, especially as it relates to the many nonclinical factors that affect certain populations disproportionately."

Leading the Pack

Of numerous examples of innovation in state Medicaid programs, Slavitt points to three in particular.

Oregon. The state received a waiver in 2012 to launch its coordinated care organization (CCO) program, which capitates regional Medicaid plans. CCOs are composed of multidisciplinary stakeholders, including health care providers, community members and at-risk health systems. Each must have a community advisory council, composed of at least 51 percent Medicaid members, that develops a community health assessment and health improvement plan (Crumley and Houston 2019). Savings from the program are reinvested in the community in a "spirit of cooperation."

North Carolina. The state received a Section 1115 demonstration waiver in late 2018 to use Medicaid funding for nonmedical purposes as part of a program called Healthy Opportunities Pilots. This program focuses on implementing evidence-based, nonmedical services that address social determinants of health (Hinton et al. 2019).

Massachusetts. MassHealth, the state's Medicaid program, contracted with 18 health care organizations—hospitals, physician networks and other health care providers—as part of its accountable care organization program that started in January 2018. The program was made possible by a $50 billion Medicaid waiver and is designed to improve health care integration and coordination while holding providers at risk for outcomes and costs (Commonwealth of Massachusetts 2017).

Conclusion

Slavitt says that Medicaid reform represents an important opportunity for hospitals and health systems—particularly safety-net organizations—to collaborate with state governments in identifying and implementing innovative solutions that will strengthen the Medicaid system for the future and better serve its beneficiaries and medical providers. "It is far better to have a strategy for making things better than to have a victim mentality," he observes. "At this pivotal juncture, the key question is how health care leaders will respond. We need them to step up and play an active and integral role in blazing the path forward for the Medicaid program."

References

Antonisse, L., R. Garfield, R. Rudowitz and S. Artiga. 2019. "The Effects of Medicaid Expansion Under the ACA: Updated Findings from a Literature Review." Kaiser Family Foundation. Published August 15. www.kff.org/medicaid/issue-brief/the-effects-of-medicaid-expansion-under-the-aca-updated-findings-from-a-literature-review-august-2019/.

Aron-Dine, A., R. Chaudhry and M. Broaddus. 2018. "Many Working People Could Lose Health Coverage Due to Medicaid Work Requirements." Center on Budget and Policy Priorities. Published April 11. www.cbpp.org/research/health/many-working-people-could-lose-health-coverage-due-to-medicaid-work-requirements.

Commonwealth of Massachusetts. 2017. "MassHealth Partners with 18 Health Care Organizations to Improve Health Care Outcomes for Members." Published June 8. www.mass.gov/news/masshealth-partners-with-18-health-care-organizations-to-improve-health-care-outcomes-for.

County Health Rankings and Roadmaps. 2019. "County Health Rankings Model." Accessed September 4. www.countyhealthrankings.org/explore-health-rankings/measures-data-sources/county-health-rankings-model.

Crumley, D. and R. Houston. 2019. "Refining Oregon's Medicaid Transformation Strategy Through CCO 2.0: A Q&A with the Oregon Health Authority." Center for Health Care Strategies. Published April 16. www.chcs.org/refining-oregons-medicaid-transformation-strategy-through-cco-2-o-a-qa-with-the-oregon-health-authority/.

Daniel-Robinson, L. and J.E. Moore. 2019. "Innovation and Opportunities to Address Social Determinants of Health in Medicaid Managed Care." Institute for Medicaid Innovation. Published January. www.medicaidinnovation.org/_images/content/2019-IMI-Social_Determinants_of_Health_in_Medicaid-Report.pdf.

Dietsche, E. 2019. "Northwell Partners with NowPow to Address Social Determinants of Health." *MedCity News*. Published June 21. https://medcitynews.com/2019/06/northwell-nowpow/.

Garfield, R., E. Hinton, E. Cornachione and C. Hall. 2018. "Medicaid Managed Care Plans and Access to Care: Results from the Kaiser Family Foundation 2017 Survey of Medicaid Managed Care Plans." Kaiser Family Foundation. Published March 5. www.kff.org/report-section/medicaid-managed-care-plans-and-access-to-care-introduction/.

Glied, S. and M. Tavenner. 2019. "Medicaid Through the Crystal Ball of Historical CMS Projections." *Health Affairs Blog*. Published February 27. www.healthaffairs.org/do/10.1377/hblog20190226.922368/full/.

Hinton, E., S. Artiga, M. Musemeci and R. Rudowitz. 2019. "A First Look at North Carolina's Section 1115 Medicaid Waiver's Healthy Opportunities Pilots." Kaiser Family Foundation. Published May 15. www.kff.org/medicaid/issue-brief/a-first-look-at-north-carolinas-section-1115-medicaid-waivers-healthy-opportunities-pilots/.

Kaiser Family Foundation. 2019. "Status of State Medicaid Expansion Decisions: Interactive Map." Published November 15. www.kff.org/medicaid/issue-brief/status-of-state-medicaid-expansion-decisions-interactive-map/.

———. 2017. "States and Medicaid Provider Taxes or Fees." Published June 27. www.kff.org/medicaid/fact-sheet/states-and-medicaid-provider-taxes-or-fees/.

Mazurenko, O., C.P. Balio, R. Agarwal, A.E. Carroll and N. Menachemi. 2018. "The Effects of Medicaid Expansion Under the ACA: A Systematic Review." *Health Affairs* 37 (6): 944–50.

Morse, S. 2018. "What Montefiore's 300% ROI from Social Determinants Investments Means for the Future of Other Hospitals." *Healthcare Finance*. Published July 5. www.healthcarefinancenews.com/news/what-montefiores-300-roi-social-determinants-investments-means-future-other-hospitals.

Pruitt, Z., N. Emechebe, T. Quast, P. Taylor and K. Bryant. 2018. "Expenditure Reductions Associated with a Social Service Referral Program." *Population Health Management* 21 (6): 469–76.

Rudowitz, R., R. Garfield and E. Hinton. 2019. "10 Things to Know About Medicaid: Setting the Facts Straight." Kaiser Family Foundation. Published March 6. www.kff.org/medicaid/issue-brief/10-things-to-know-about-medicaid-setting-the-facts-straight/.

Slavitt, A. 2018. "Work Requirements for Health Coverage." *Journal of the American Medical Association* 320 (8): 746–47.

Society for Health Care Strategy & Market Development
Executive director: Diane Weber, RN
Managing editor: Brian Griffin
Senior research data analytics specialist: Ann Feeney

The Society for Health Care Strategy & Market Development (SHSMD) of the American Hospital Association is the largest and most prominent voice for health care strategists in marketing, planning, business development, communications and public relations. SHSMD is committed to leading, connecting, and serving its members to prepare them for the future with greater knowledge and opportunity as their organizations strive to improve the health of their communities. The society provides a broad and constantly updated array of resources, services, experiences and connections.

SHSMD leaders are available for on-site presentations about *Futurescan 2020–2025* to health care governing boards, senior management, planning teams and medical staffs. To arrange for a leadership presentation, contact SHSMD at 312.422.3888 or shsmd@aha.org.

American College of Healthcare Executives/Health Administration Press
President and CEO: Deborah J. Bowen, FACHE, CAE
Director, Health Administration Press: Michael E. Cunningham, CAE
Project manager: Andrew J. Baumann

The American College of Healthcare Executives is an international professional society of more than 48,000 healthcare executives who lead hospitals, healthcare systems and other healthcare organizations. ACHE's mission is to advance our members and healthcare management excellence. ACHE offers its prestigious FACHE® credential, signifying board certification in healthcare management. ACHE's established network of 77 chapters provides access to networking, education and career development at the local level. In addition, ACHE is known for its magazine, *Healthcare Executive*, and its career development and public policy programs. Through such efforts, ACHE works toward its vision of being the preeminent professional society for leaders dedicated to improving health.

The Foundation of the American College of Healthcare Executives was established to further advance healthcare management excellence through education and research. The Foundation of ACHE is known for its educational programs—including the annual Congress on Healthcare Leadership, which draws more than 4,000 participants—and groundbreaking research. Its publishing division, Health Administration Press, is one of the largest publishers of books and journals on health services management, including textbooks for college and university courses. For more information, visit www.ache.org.

ABOUT THE SPONSOR

The American Hospital Association (AHA) is a not-for-profit association of health care provider organizations and individuals that are committed to the improvement of health in their communities. The AHA is the national advocate for its members, which include nearly 5,000 hospitals, health care systems, networks and other providers of care. Founded in 1898, the AHA provides education for health care leaders and is a source of information on health care issues and trends. For more information, visit www.aha.org.